Adopting
a child
The definitive guide to adoption in England, Wales and Northern Ireland

Jenifer Lord

coramBAAF
ADOPTION & FOSTERING ACADEMY

Published by
CoramBAAF Adoption and Fostering Academy
41 Brunswick Square
London WC1N 1AZ
www.corambaaf.org.uk

Coram Academy Limited registered as a company
limited by guarantee in England and Wales
number 9697712, part of the Coram group,
charity number 312278

British Library Cataloguing in Publication Data
A catalogue record for this book is available from
the British Library

ISBN 978 1 910039 53 3

Cover design: mecob.org
Cover photograph: © Siri Stafford/Getty Images
All photographs posed by models
Designed by Helen Joubert Designs
Typeset by Fravashi Aga
Printed in Great Britain by T J International

Contents

Acknowledgements

The first four editions of *Adopting A Child* were co-authored by Prue Chennells and Chris Hammond in 1984, 1986, 1990 and 1995. Jenifer Lord made considerable revisions for the fifth edition in 1998, and in subsequent editions. This edition has been revised by Isabelle Rameau. It draws on the previous editions but has been revised and updated in light of legislative changes.

2013 edition: Thanks to John Simmonds, BAAF, for helpful information on current practice; Katrina Wilson, BAAF, and Andy Stott, Adoption Register for England and Wales, for their efficient help with statistical information; Catherine Mullin, BAAF Northern Ireland, for helpful information in relation to Northern Ireland; and Jo Francis, Publications Department, BAAF, for her work in producing this edition.

The 2016 edition has been revised by Isabelle Rameau, with thanks to Katrina Wilson, CoramBAAF, for help with statistical information.

The quotations in this book have been taken from several sources, including personal communication and a number of BAAF and CoramBAAF books, which can be found in Useful Reading or in the Bookshop at www.corambaaf.org.uk.

Note about the author

Jenifer Lord was for many years a child placement consultant who worked in BAAF's Southern England office. She is also the author of *The Adoption Process in England*, and has co-authored *Effective Adoption Panels, Effective Fostering Panels* and *Together or Apart? Assessing siblings for permanent placement*.

Becoming an adoptive parent

The journey to become adoptive parents does not start from the same place, or finish in the same place, for all people…My journey began with the long-held expectation that I would become a father. The next chapter of the journey was the recognition that this was not happening, followed by the realisation that it was not going to.

Unlike others, we elected not to go the IVF route, we did consider adoption but didn't pursue it at the time. Instead, the next twist in the tale was relaxing with our fate and becoming happy and content as two.

Looking at adoption had sown a seed though, and we couldn't help but think that all those positives we had for two were there to share with a third. We had loving hearts and a home to share and there might be a child out there who could benefit from that.

So, with undecided minds we set the ball rolling, the plan being to learn more so that we could make our decision. The adoption preparation course did just that; we learned of the children who are in care needing families and the issues they face.

There were fears that seemed like risks: I was aware of some of the effects of trauma in childhood and of the challenges, and the challenging behaviour, that it could bring. There were also hopes: that we would make a real difference for a little person and get to experience the joys that being a parent brings.

The assessment process proved to be not just us being evaluated, it was an education and reassurance. It answered many questions, explored many issues, agreed and defined our limits and made us aware of the support we could draw upon to make this union a successful one.

Adoption isn't for everyone, but it's more accessible than many might think. It's certainly a journey that requires a bit of bravery and tenacity to bring to fruition – and of course you live with your child's background, just as they do.

So fast forward to our present day and we now share our lives with a beautiful baby girl – and we love each other. We are immersed in the joys and anxieties of parenthood – and it's amazing.

I doubt I will do anything more worthwhile in my lifetime.

Stephen, adoptive dad, CoramBAAF blog

Introduction

*Sometimes you feel really scared because you never know if
your new parents will be as kind as you want them to be.
Sometimes you'll feel really happy because your old parents
were mean to you and you're glad to get a new start to life.
Sometimes it's most scary because you're only young and you
are not used to moving. But you'll always feel a sigh of relief
when everything goes really well.*

Different feelings you feel on being adopted, by Jessica,
age 9, *The Colours in Me*

Around 5,500 children are currently adopted each year in the UK.*
Over 90 per cent of these are children who have been looked after by
a local authority. The others are predominantly children adopted by
their parent and step-parent, and about 100–150 are children who
have been brought from overseas and adopted by people living in the
UK. There is a chapter in this book that focuses on step-families
considering adoption, and one that focuses on people considering
adopting from overseas. The rest of this book is about the adoption

* Figures are estimated, based on information available from different parts of
the UK. There are some variations in the detail of what is collected and the most
recent figures available but efforts have been made to ensure that the overall
picture is realistic.

of children who are looked after by local authorities. There is also a chapter on meeting these children's needs through fostering.

There are currently nearly 93,500 children looked after by local authorities in the UK, 70 per cent of whom (around 64,600) live in foster homes. Many looked after children will return home to their family within a year.

The number of looked after children who are adopted represents a tiny proportion, just over 6.5 per cent, of all looked after children. Over 75 per cent of the looked after children adopted recently in England were aged between one and four. This reflects the wishes of many adopters to parent preschool children and the relative ease with which adoption agencies are able to recruit adopters for young children. It doesn't reflect the needs of many waiting children for whom new families are urgently needed.

Children who wait for adoption tend to be older. There are single children but many are in groups of brothers and sisters who need placement together. There are children with disabilities who range in age from babies upwards. There are children from a huge variety of ethnic, religious and cultural backgrounds. Many of the children have been abused and/or neglected before they are taken into local authority care and they will have been further confused and upset by uncertainty and moves after coming into care.

Just as there is a wide range of children needing adoption, so will a wide range of people be welcomed by adoption agencies to adopt them. People of every ethnic, religious and cultural background, couples and single people – heterosexual as well as lesbian and gay, both with or without children – older people, people who have been divorced, all can and do become successful adoptive parents. And the great majority of adoptions work out well. Like all parents, adoptive parents get huge joy and satisfaction from parenting their children, as well as finding it very hard work and sometimes frustrating and painful.

Traditionally, adoption, for children not previously known to the families adopting them, was seen as severing connections with the past and starting afresh. Now it is understood how important it is to provide adoptive parents with as much information as possible to pass on to their children, and how important their heritage is for those children. Many adopted children continue to maintain important relationships – sometimes with their birth parents, more often with other family members like brothers and sisters, grandparents, aunts and uncles.

Adoption agencies do not expect you to know all about adoption before you approach them. They will provide information and opportunities for you to find out about what will be involved, for instance, by introducing you to experienced adoptive parents. They are also working hard to provide better help and support to you and your child once you are living together and after you have adopted. Help is also available from adoptive parents' support groups and, in England and Wales, from post-adoption centres.

We hope that this book will answer most of your initial questions as well as clarify anything that may have previously puzzled you about adoption – the processes, the cost, the legal issues, etc. All these and many other issues are addressed in this book. These are illustrated with real-life experiences in which people candidly talk about what went right and what went wrong, and how they were helped or helped themselves to create a safe, secure and loving family environment for a child or children who needed this. For children who have to be separated from their birth families, having a new permanent family by adoption is an experience that must fulfil their needs and help them through to a fulfilling adulthood.

A glossary of terms that are used in this book and which may be unfamiliar to you is provided at the end.

Adoption legislation

The Adoption and Children Act 2002 was fully implemented in England and Wales in December 2005. It is underpinned by more than 10 sets of regulations and also by Statutory Guidance.

There are National Minimum Standards for adoption work in England and Wales. These standards form the basis for inspection of adoption services.

Your local adoption agency will be able to give you up-to-date information and there are links to the Standards and legislation at www.corambaaf.org.uk.

Adoption is changing and developing and it will be important for you to check with a local adoption agency about any significant changes at the time you make your initial enquiries.

Scope of this edition

The content of this edition applies to England, where some new adoption regulations and statutory guidance were introduced in 2013. Much of it also applies to Wales, and quite a lot to Northern Ireland, although recognising that there are variations between the different countries.

If you live in Scotland and are interested in adoption, *Adopting a Child in Scotland*, for prospective adopters living in Scotland, will be more relevant to you (available from CoramBAAF).

Adoption as a legal process was first established in 1926 in England and Wales, in 1929 in Northern Ireland, and in 1930 in Scotland. Although these are separate jurisdictions, the legal framework for adoption was very similar and was primarily about legal security for babies relinquished by their birth parents. Now that most children placed for adoption with non-relatives have spent a period looked after by the local authority, planning for them must also take account of other child care legislation.

There is one Adoption and Children Act for England and Wales but separate regulations. Northern Ireland has tended to look towards England and Wales in developing its legislation.

However, there are some differences in practice and procedures.

In Northern Ireland there are still a small number of babies who come into or are removed to care at a very early age and proceed to adoption. Adoption as a route out of care for older children in Northern Ireland continues to be developed.

As stated previously, much of the text that follows will be relevant to England, Wales and Northern Ireland but more information about local variations can be obtained from your local adoption agency. The legislation provides for children moving from one legal jurisdiction to another so that children can be linked with families across the UK.

Just as the law has been updated over the 80-plus years that legal adoption has been possible, so practice has changed tremendously. The rest of this book will tell you more about this. One aspect of this that affects the delivery of adoption services is the change in local government. At first, much of the adoption service was provided by voluntary adoption agencies. Now there are fewer such agencies and most children placed are the responsibility of their local authority children's services, which also act as adoption agencies to recruit and prepare adopters. A number of councils have been looking at different ways of delivering services. Children's services may now be joined with education or housing services so that where reference is made to children's services or Directors, you may need to check the precise names/designations locally. Although these terms are not accurate when applied to Northern Ireland, we have used them for the sake of simplicity. In Northern Ireland, children's services are provided by Health and Social Care Trusts.

We adopted our three fabulous children nearly two-and-a-half years ago now. At the time they were three, four and nearly six years old. Why did we adopt a sibling group? The most obvious reason was that we had always wanted a big family and it seemed logical to us that if we were going to adopt more than one child then it would be nice if they came together and had a shared history. Maybe a less obvious, but probably more emotive, reason was that we both have fond memories of growing up with our own siblings. When we read that sibling groups that cannot find adoptive placements together can be placed separately, it really broke our hearts. And finally we felt that we had so much love and devotion to give to our "prospective children" that we were likely to overwhelm just one child!

Adopters, CoramBAAF website

1

Children needing adoption

I was adopted when I was small…I am glad I am adopted, although adoption brings with it feelings of loss, sadness, anger and many, many more feelings, it also brings great joy and happiness to everyone involved. I would like to say thank you to my family for adopting me and for being the best ever. I love them so much. They have changed my life so much for the better. I could never describe how much.

When I am older, maybe when I am a granny, after I have been a policewoman and a mummy and a sailing instructor for disabled children, I would like to be able to give other children another chance in life like I was given. I think it is a lovely thing to do as children also have feelings which are valid and should be recognised, and every child deserves to be loved no matter who they are or what they are like. Every child is special and worth something in the world.

Julia, age 14, *The Colours in Me*

Just over 2,000 children currently in the care system in England could be placed for adoption with families if the families were available. Although the children are very different, they all have one thing in common: a need for a family.

It is recognised that, for nearly all children, life in a family is best. A new family can bring love and security to the child – and a child can bring joy and satisfaction to the family. Every child is different and brings the potential for different sorts of satisfaction just as they will bring their own set of needs and challenges.The adoption agency's job, with your help, is to match that child's potential and needs with your abilities and expectations.

Are there any babies needing adoption?

Of around 5,500 children adopted in the UK in the year to March 2016, around 250 were babies under one. Today it is easier for women to choose to parent on their own and fewer single mothers are placing their babies for adoption. Contraception is more efficient than it used to be, and fewer unplanned pregnancies occur. It is also easier to terminate pregnancies than previously.

There are more white people interested in adopting a white baby without disabilities than there are such babies needing adoption. Agencies have little difficulty in finding suitable adopters for white babies without disabilities. This means that people who want to adopt only such a child are likely to find it hard even to get started on the adoption process and may not be able to adopt a baby.

However, agencies are somewhat less successful at finding black families or those from other minority ethnic groups, although they are getting better at it. This means that if you and/or your partner are black or from a minority ethnic group, you are more likely to find an agency to take up your application quite quickly. You will probably have a shorter wait before being linked with a baby, although this will vary as only quite small numbers of black babies and those from other minority ethnic groups are placed for adoption each year. If you can consider older children, your wait could be shorter.

I was aware of the high proportion of black children in the care system, and a real need for black carers to come forward to adopt them. I'm black British of Jamaican origin, so this struck a chord.

Adoptive mum

There are babies with disabilities or disabling conditions such as cerebral palsy and Foetal Alcohol Spectrum Disorder who need to be adopted. There are also some babies with genetic factors in their background, such as schizophrenia or Huntington's Chorea, for whom it is not always easy to find adoptive families.

Toddlers and preschool children

Children aged between one and five are the largest group of children adopted in the UK. This reflects the wishes of many adopters to parent preschool children and the relative ease with which adoption agencies are able to recruit adopters for young children. The majority of these placements work out extremely successfully. However, these children often have complex needs. They may have been abused and neglected and given little opportunity to make attachments to reliable parent figures. They may be very confused about all that has happened in their short lives and unable to trust in anyone. In addition, there may also be uncertainties about their development which may not be resolved until they are older. Families need to be able to take on these issues and to access support and advice.

What about older children?

Many children waiting to be adopted are aged five or over. They may have lived for some years with one or both of their parents, or other family members, or they may have had many moves in and out of foster homes, and the damage done by these experiences can last a very long time. Older children need especially resilient parents who can help them face up to the past – including their possible need to keep in touch with some members of their family – and see them through the difficult adolescent years to maturity. In a loving and secure home, most of these children will eventually begin to thrive, although the older they are, the longer it may take.

Being adopted is great because you know who you are with a family who cares for you and loves you very much. I know it may be hard to leave your parents but you know they can't look after you, but they can write to you and they will always love you.

Rebecca, age 11, *The Colours in Me*

Children who have been looked after by a local authority for months or years are likely to have emotional and behavioural problems because of the experiences which led to them having to be separated from their birth families, but also because of not having a permanent parent figure in their lives. Even young children soon learn that there isn't much point in getting attached to an adult who is soon going to disappear out of their lives. They may find it difficult to become attached to a new family and are likely to test out their new parents with challenging behaviour. Young children may be more like babies in their behaviour sometimes, and even teenagers may act like very young children. But most children of all ages can eventually settle when they realise that they really are part of the family.

There are children who have been so hurt by their past experiences that they will go on having special needs throughout their childhood, even though they have clearly benefited from becoming a loved member of the family. If you adopt a child who is likely to have particular ongoing needs, you should ensure as far as possible that the agency will make arrangements for them to have any special help they may continue to require on a long-term basis.

The other thing about adopting older children is that you know if there are any medical issues or developmental issues. A lot of the issues that affect children in care will be evident, whereas if they are a year old, you might not know.

Adopter, *The Pink Guide to Adoption*

Groups of brothers and sisters

Around half of all the children waiting for adoptive families in England are in groups of brothers and sisters needing to be placed together. Most of these children are in groups of two, although there are some groups of three or more. Brothers and sisters can provide support and comfort for each other throughout their lives. If they want to stay together and if an assessment of their needs has shown that one family could parent them successfully, it is very sad if they have to be separated because no families come forward for them all. You may be daunted by the practicalities, but extra help and support could and should be available (see Chapter 5). Brothers and sisters share a family history and can support each other in making sense of what has happened to them. Research indicates that, compared to children of the same age placed on their own, brothers and sisters placed together are likely to do as well or better.

There can be rivalry and spats, and their perception sometimes is that they "hate" each other! But it's obvious that having each other is a tremendous reassurance. It is the only constant and stable thing they've had in their lives.

Adopters of three brothers

Disabled children or children who have complex needs

Many children waiting to be placed for adoption have special needs that can range from health conditions, to learning or physical disabilities, and emotional or behavioural difficulties. For some children, their future development may be uncertain, or they may be too young for a prognosis to be made.

A disability can be anything from autism to Down's syndrome, cerebral palsy to a visual impairment, and each child will be affected and respond differently.

Disabled children or children with complex needs may be placed for adoption at a very young age because their parents feel unable to care for them. They may be looked after by the local authority after their parents have tried unsuccessfully to cope. So they may feel the impact both of their disability, the loss of their family of origin, and perhaps the confusion of a residential setting where different staff come and go. People who adopt these children will need to be prepared for a challenging yet rewarding task, as some of the children may never be able to lead entirely independent lives. In some cases, experience of disability in prospective adopters – either their own personal or professional experience or that of their children – will be positively welcomed.

Learning disabilities/difficulties, special educational needs

There are many babies and older children who have learning difficulties/disabilities waiting for adoption, for example, children with Foetal Alcohol Spectrum Disorder. These are children who, as well as individual love and care, need additional help and support to enable them to participate in as many as possible of the experiences and opportunities open to any other child.

There are many children whose learning disabilities are not clear-cut: they may have suffered an accident or injury while very young which has affected their ability to learn or to understand the world around them – but no one knows how much. Or they may have been born with a disability that isn't clear to doctors. They may have been chronically neglected and/or abused as a baby and young child, and the extent of the damage this has caused and the possibility of change may still be unclear.

Many of the children will have special educational needs and may need to receive additional support at school, such as speech and language therapy or extra help from a teacher or assistant. Some children may have missed out on some of their education, or find it difficult to learn and concentrate. If the child's needs cannot be met by the resources of their school, it may be in their best interests to attend a different type of school, perhaps one that provides a more specialist education.

Our fourth birth child taught us not to be afraid of disability. She was born with Edward's Syndrome, and through this we became aware of the disabled children left in hospital because their parents found it too difficult to cope. So we decided to adopt.

Adoptive mum of two disabled children, *Could you be my Parent?*

Physical disabilities

There are many types of physical disability – cerebral palsy, muscular dystrophy, spina bifida and cystic fibrosis are just some of them. Children with these disabilities need the love and security that life in a family offers just as much as other children do. And, like most children, they will give love and affection in return. Having a physical disability does not mean having a learning disability too, although people sometimes confuse the two. People with physical disabilities can lead increasingly independent lives nowadays – especially if they have the support of a loving family.

Developmental delay/developmental uncertainty

Children who fall behind the progress made by most other children of their age are said to be delayed in their physical, emotional, intellectual or educational development. Where this delay is due to past experiences of disruptions or lack of care or stimulation, it may be temporary. It can also last longer. For some children, their delay may be linked to learning or physical impairments.

With some children there is a level of uncertainty over their future development. This uncertainty may be based on the knowledge that their birth mother used drugs or alcohol during pregnancy, or that one birth parent has a condition such as, for instance, schizophrenia, which the child may inherit or develop at a later stage. For some children, especially if they are very young, a precise developmental assessment hasn't been carried out yet and there is no clear diagnosis or prognosis.

Emotional and behavioural needs

It is common for many children needing adoption to have previously experienced lack of care, lack of supervision, including neglect, or physical, emotional or sexual abuse, as well as separation and loss from their birth family. The majority of the children waiting for new families, including babies and infants, will have specific emotional needs due to their early life experiences.

Many children, particularly those who have had more than one carer, will have emotional or behavioural issues, such as attachment difficulties. Attachment is the process of emotional bonding between babies and their main carers, which is usually the mother, in the first few years of life. Research indicates that missing out on this connection can affect a child's social behaviour and emotional development.

Many children can find it hard to "recover" from their early difficult experiences, even with lots of love and attention from their adoptive family. Some children benefit from therapy or other types of support. Some children's needs are best met when they are the youngest or only child in their adoptive family.

Are children from different ethnic backgrounds waiting to be adopted?

Yes, there are children from a great variety of ethnic, cultural and religious backgrounds waiting for adoption. They all need families who will cherish and value their heritage and identity; families who either match their ethnicity, culture, religion and language as closely as possible, or who can actively promote these aspects of their identity.

Do the children all have contact with their birth families?

It depends on what is meant by contact. It can mean anything from an adoption where the child has regular face-to-face – known as "direct" – contact with members of his or her birth family to an adoption where the adopters have met the birth parents once and there is an annual letter exchanged via the adoption agency, called "indirect" or "letterbox" contact. Many children being placed for adoption now will have a plan for their adoptive parents to have at least an annual exchange of news with their birth family via the adoption agency. Others will need and want to meet members of their birth family, sometimes grandparents, brothers and sisters, and occasionally their parents, perhaps once or twice a year.

Contact must be planned to meet the child's needs. These will change over time and everyone involved needs to be prepared to be flexible. Contact can be very positive and can result in a child being more rather than less settled in their new family. Contact can sometimes be easier for everyone to manage if the child's adopters match their heritage as closely as possible. You will need to be clear what the plan for contact is for any child whom you plan to adopt.

Our twin boys joined us when they were three…Direct contact is planned with their other siblings twice a year. The boys don't have memories of living with them so we are going into the unknown, but so far their relationships seem very positive. We talk about their siblings and have photos around the home.

Adopter

2

Who can adopt?

When I arrived at the foster family's home, I trembled as I knocked on the door. We said hello and then suddenly there was little Alan, bright as a button and very excited. 'Who's this?', the carer asked. 'It's Mummy,' cried Alan. When I remember that moment, in my head it's like one of those romantic wedding pictures that you see, where the couple are in the centre of the picture and they're framed by a sort of blurry line…The truth is that he came running to the door, with a bottle of sugary drink dripping all over him. He had something horrible and sticky all round his mouth and his nappy, a frankly rather stinky one, was hanging off him. Somehow, although it must have registered somewhere in my memory, I didn't notice that at the time. Love at first sight? Yes, I think so.

Julia Wise, single adopter, *Flying Solo*

Are there long waiting lists for adopters?

It is estimated that at any one time, there are just over 2,000 children looked after by local authorities in England who are waiting to be adopted (with a Placement Order). Adopters of all ages, with or without children already, both couples and single people, are urgently needed to offer them a chance of family life. There is often a mismatch between the children who need an adoptive family and the kind of children people want to adopt, which can result in families having to wait to be matched with a child. It is worth thinking about the kinds of children you are willing to consider, such as groups of brothers and sisters, older children or children with developmental delay or complex needs, to widen your opportunities to be matched more quickly.

Do I have to be "special" to adopt?

No, but understanding, energy, commitment, and the ability to face up to challenges and difficulties will all be needed.

Just as you will be providing support and understanding to a child with a variety of different needs, so you will need support yourself. Your family, including your children if you have any, plus your close relatives and friends, need to be in agreement with your plan, because you will almost certainly call on them for help. Your immediate family will, like yourself, be very closely affected. Children who have been hurt by their experiences can hurt others in their search for security.

If your family isn't on your side from the beginning, the whole process will be much more difficult. Even before the adoption process starts, it's essential that the support network is there – especially from your family...The child has to grow up with your relatives, as well as you.

Adopter

You will need all the help you can get. In return, though, you will get the joy and satisfaction of seeing some of the emotional damage to a child gradually start to heal. The rest of this chapter gives information on issues which you may be concerned or unsure about. The adoption agencies that you contact will also give you written information on their eligibility criteria for prospective adopters.

Are there age limits?

You have to be at least 21 years old to adopt in law (unless you are a birth parent involved in a joint step-parent adoption, in which case the age is 18).

There is a greater health risk as people age. Agencies have a responsibility to ensure as far as possible that prospective adopters are likely to be fit and active at least until their child is a young adult. Although there is no upper age limit, many agencies would not usually expect there to be more than about a 45-year age gap between the child and their adoptive parents. However, this is flexible and depends partly on what the adopters are offering in relation to the needs of waiting children. The average age of adopters is around 40.

Birth mothers placing infants for adoption often ask for their child to be placed with parents within average childbearing ages. So, if agencies are considering adopters for babies for whom there is a huge choice of families, they may decide to work with slightly younger people.

> *We were well into our forties and had already been married for about 15 years when we decided to adopt a child. We already had three birth children and had made sure we couldn't have any more! To many of our friends it seemed an odd decision, taken at the stage in life when most parents are beginning to think about the time when their children will leave the nest!*

Adopters

Do I have to be married?

You can adopt if you are:

- single;
- married (same-sex and opposite sex);
- in a civil partnership;
- an unmarried couple (same-sex and opposite sex);
- the partner of the child's parent.

All couples, whether married, unmarried or in a civil partnership, and regardless of their sexual orientation, can adopt jointly.

People who have been divorced can adopt. If you are married or in a partnership, adoption agencies may prefer you to have been together for a year or more before taking up an adoption application from you.

> *We were enthusiastic and honest. We told her that we had had problems in our marriage and gone for counselling, and she was very positive about it.*

Jasminder, adoptive mum, *Looking After our Own*

Do I have to be British?

No. You are eligible to adopt a child in the UK if your permanent home is in the UK (the legal term is "domicile") or if you have been habitually resident in the UK for at least a year. If you are adopting as a couple, only one of you needs to be domiciled or both of you need to be habitually resident. Habitual residence is quite a difficult status to define and you may need to take legal advice on whether you qualify. You will need to be resident in the UK for long enough to be assessed and approved as adopters, to have a child placed with you and to apply for the adoption order in court. This could take at least two years and possibly longer.

Most children needing adoption will already have had a number of moves. They are likely to be insecure and to need as much stability as possible. They may also have some ongoing contact with members of their birth family. For these reasons it may not be appropriate for many children to be placed with adopters who will be moving around a lot or living overseas after the child's adoption.

What if I'm British but working abroad for a few years?

Unless you are making arrangements for the adoption of a child already well known to you, you will almost certainly not be able to adopt a child in the UK until you return to live here.

You usually need, for practical purposes, to be living in the UK for at least two years, so that the adoption agency has a chance to work with you and get to know you, and also to match you with a child and to introduce and place the child. This is followed by a period of at least ten weeks, before you can apply for an Adoption Order. It is not until you have an Adoption Order that you will be able to take the child to live abroad with you.

What if I am disabled or in poor health?

Medical conditions or disability will not necessarily rule you out. All prospective adopters have to have a full medical examination done by their GP. The adoption agency employs a doctor who acts as a medical adviser. He or she will want your permission to contact consultants who have treated you. The adoption agency's prime concern is that you will have the health and vigour necessary to meet the needs of your child until he or she is a young adult.

What about lifestyle issues like smoking?

There is evidence that smoking causes health problems for smokers and that passive smoking can damage the health of others, particularly young children. For this reason, many agencies will not usually place pre-school children with people who smoke.

E-cigarettes, or vaping, have become more common in recent years, and are recognised as being less of a health hazard than smoking, although research into their effects is still ongoing. You will need to find out from the adoption agency you approach what position they take on this subject, and whether they are happy to consider adopters who use e-cigarettes.

Excessive alcohol consumption also leads to health problems. It may also be associated, for children in care, with violence and physical abuse. Your social worker will therefore be discussing your drinking habits with you.

There is also evidence that obesity can cause health problems, as can anorexia or other eating disorders, and so these conditions will be carefully considered by the agency.

What if I've got a criminal record?

People with a record of offences against children or who are known to have harmed children cannot be considered by adoption agencies. A criminal record of other offences need not rule you out. However, the nature of the offence and how long ago it was committed will have to be carefully considered. It is important to be open and honest with the adoption agency early on if you have a criminal record. The information will come to light when the police and other checks are done and any attempt at deception by you will be taken very seriously. Criminal records checks will also be made for all members of your household aged 18 or over in England and Wales and 10 or over in Northern Ireland.

What about finances and housing?

You do not have to own your own home or be wealthy. Adoption agencies prefer there to be a spare bedroom available for a child. However, this isn't a legal requirement and an adopted child could share a bedroom with a child already in your family. Your child would obviously need to be happy about this and it would be helpful if you had a contingency plan in case the children really didn't get on with sharing. You may be eligible to receive financial support from the local authority in certain circumstances, such as if the child whom you wish to adopt has special needs and if you could not afford to adopt him or her otherwise. (Adoption support is described in more detail in Chapter 5.)

Adopters are needed from all backgrounds – it is for everybody. I don't have my own home, a lot of money or a partner but I do have time, energy and unconditional love for this little boy, my son. It's about having the capacity to take on the challenge.

Adoptive mum

Does it matter if we're still having treatment for infertility?

You can certainly get written information from adoption agencies and also attend an information session or ask for an individual interview to find out about adoption. However, you will then need to decide whether to continue with infertility treatment or to pursue adoption. Adoption agencies will not usually be prepared to embark on a full adoption assessment and preparation with you while you are still actively involved in infertility treatment. It can be very difficult to pursue two different routes to parenting at the same time. Experience shows that most people need to end treatment and "mourn" the birth child whom they are not going to have before moving on to think positively about all the issues involved in adoption.

We'd like to adopt a child the same age as our son/daughter so that they can grow up together

There is quite a lot of research evidence that shows that it is more likely that things will not work if a child joining a family is close in age to a child already there. Agencies, therefore, often prefer to have an age difference of two years or more between children. It is also often easier for your children and for the new child if he or she can join your family as the youngest child. However, it is possible for children to come in as the eldest or as a middle child, so do discuss this with the adoption agency if you feel it might work in your family.

I'd like to be considered for children from any ethnic background

The Adoption and Children Act 2002 states that 'In placing the child for adoption, the adoption agency must give due consideration to the child's religious persuasion, racial origin and cultural and linguistic background.'

There are more white children than any other group needing adoption and so it makes sense for white families to adopt white children whose particular needs they can meet as fully as possible.

We have to accept the fact that racism is still common in Britain today. So black and minority ethnic (BME) children, including those of mixed (BME and white) heritage who will probably be identified as BME – will, sooner or later, have to cope with some form of discrimination. A black or minority ethnic child who faces racist abuse outside the home is likely to find it easier to discuss what has happened, understand it, and learn how to deal with it from a black or minority ethnic adopter who can immediately relate to this experience. Coping with racism is something white people are not so geared to, whereas for BME adults it is a fact of life. Black and minority ethnic children need this level of support in their daily life.

These children also need black and minority ethnic adults they can look up to and with whom they can identify positively. For BME children who have been unable to stay with their own families and who are then placed in white families, it can be hard to correct the false impression that white is better than black.

Matching ethnicity, religion, culture and language between a child and their adoptive family is likely to make it easier for the child to settle, may help facilitate any continuing birth family contact, and will have the long-term advantage of the child learning naturally and easily about his or her heritage.

Agencies are much more successful now at placing children with adopters who reflect their ethnicity. However, when this isn't possible without delay for the child, adopters will be sought who will cherish and value the child's heritage and identity and do all they can to promote it. This is likely to be easier for adopters who live in an ethnically diverse area and who have contacts with people who share the child's ethnicity, culture, religion and language of origin.

It doesn't really matter what other people think. I know who I am...I can say proudly that I'm half Scottish and half Indian and that my nationality is British and Australian and that I was raised by white, English parents...It always makes for an interesting conversation when someone asks me where I'm from and I now have the choice as to how much I wish to disclose.

Adopted adult, *In Search of Belonging*

Statutory Guidance on Adoption published by the Department for Education in 2013 states that:

A prospective adopter can be matched with a child with whom they do not share the same ethnicity, provided they can meet the child's other identified needs. The core issue is what qualities, experiences and attributes the prospective adopter can draw on and their level of understanding of the discrimination and racism the child may be confronted with when growing up.

And that:

If the prospective adopter can meet most of the child's needs, the social worker must not delay placing a child with the prospective adopter because they are single, older than other adopters or does not share the child's racial or cultural background.

I'm worried about an open adoption. Will this rule me out?

It depends what you mean by an open adoption. The term is used to mean anything from a one-off meeting with your child's birth parents and an annual exchange of news via the adoption agency to regular face-to-face contact between your child and members of their birth family. It is recognised now that it can be helpful for some children to maintain some face-to-face contact, perhaps with a grandparent or a brother or sister placed elsewhere and sometimes with their birth parents. Face-to-face contact is not the plan for all children and you can discuss with the agency if you do not wish to be linked to a child who needs this contact.

However, all adoptive parents need to have an open attitude to their child's birth family and past. You need to recognise the importance of this for your child and be prepared to talk with your child about his or her often confused feelings about their birth family and their past. You also have to accept that things can change and that your child may want direct contact in the future even though that isn't the plan now.

I perhaps sometimes don't really want to acknowledge the fact that he's adopted. I wish he was mine, my biological…so, yeah…but I'm very conscious that it's something that we need to be very open about, you know, so that he is prepared for the future and knows as much as possible.

Adoptive mum, *Gay, Lesbian and Heterosexual Adoptive Families*

A one-off meeting with birth parents can be very valuable in helping you talk with your child about their birth family and it can be reassuring for the child to know that you have met his or her birth parents. Most adoption agencies would expect you to be prepared for a one-off meeting. They would also expect that you could consider at least an annual exchange of news, usually anonymously via the adoption agency, with your child's birth parents.

If you are critical of the people who are part of your child's make-up, then you are rejecting part of them. But if you accept and empathise with the past then you can make a good life for your child. The gains are enormous.

Adoptive mum, *Could you be my Parent?*

Can I adopt my foster child?

This is discussed in Chapter 8.

Can I adopt a member of my family?

The law allows a child to be placed for adoption by a parent with the child's brother, sister, uncle, aunt or grandparent, without this needing to be agreed by an adoption agency.

For a child who is unable to live with his or her birth parents, living with a member of their extended family may well be the next best thing. However, there are other ways to give the child security which you could also consider. For instance, a Special Guardianship Order, a Child Arrangements Order (in England and Wales) or a Residence Order (in Northern Ireland) give the carers parental responsibility without taking this away from the birth parents and cutting the child off from them legally, as an Adoption Order does. If you are considering adopting a family member, you may find it helpful to talk this through with a social worker from the local authority where you live, before you apply. There is more information on these Orders in Chapter 8.

If you decide to go ahead with the adoption you can start the process for applying to court. The Adoption and Children Act 2002 for England and Wales requires that at least three months before applying to a court to adopt, you must notify the social services department of the local authority where you live of your intention to apply. The Act also requires that the child must have lived with you for at least three years out of the last five before you apply. However, you can apply to court for permission to make an application sooner. You can apply to your local Magistrates' Family Proceedings Court, County Court or the High Court.

The local authority must prepare a comprehensive report for the court. This will involve interviews with you, the child and the child's parents, who will need to consent to the adoption. Medical reports and checks will need to be done. Should the child's parents decide to withdraw their agreement at this stage, the court can consider dispensing with it, if there is compelling evidence to do so.

If a child in your family is already being looked after by the local authority and seems unlikely to return to his or her parents and you would like to consider offering the child a permanent home, you should contact the child's social worker or local authority as soon as possible. They will welcome your interest.

It's stating the obvious, but it's a fact: adoption changes your life! You can't just absorb a child into your family without changing your lifestyle. You have to give up certain things, you have to make financial adjustments, you have to cope with emotional pressures and deal with changing relationships. I think we grossly underestimated the impact adoption would have on our lives.

Adoptive dad, *The Family Business*

3

How do I get approved to adopt a child?

I'd always fancied adoption...We received something from the council by chance, that had a postage advert on it saying, 'Could you adopt?' Around that time, I also saw an advertisement on the back of a bus and read an article in The Guardian newspaper. This all prompted us to go to an open evening. Thirteen months later our children moved in.

The [application and assessment] process was quite easy. I think if you go into it with a positive attitude, it helps. We were open and enjoyed the training courses. We made some good friends. There were two gay men on the course [as well as the two of us]. Generally, we sailed through it and were allocated a lovely social worker. There were one or two moments when I felt like a jellyfish, answering questions that made me feel awkward. You have to accept that social workers are doing their job and have to get it right.

Kate and Sophie, adopters, *Proud Parents*

First steps

It can be helpful to do some reading about adoption as it is today and about the kind of children needing families before you approach an adoption agency. This book is a good start and other useful reading is listed at the end.

Many people thinking about adoption also find it invaluable to speak to experienced adopters. Adoption UK is a self-help group for adoptive and prospective adoptive parents before, during and after adoption. It has local groups throughout the UK which you could join and whose members will be pleased to talk to you (see Useful Organisations).

If you live in England, you could also contact First4Adoption, a national contact point for information which includes e-learning material – www.first4adoption.org.uk. If you live in Wales, you could contact the National Adoption Service, which fulfils a similar function – www.adoptcymru.com.

Contacting an agency

This important step is fully covered in Chapter 10.

Can I respond to children I see featured through a family-finding service before I contact a local agency?

Yes, you can. Social workers featuring children through family-finding services such as Children who Wait or Link Maker, in local newspapers and other media are happy to hear from unapproved families. However, their priority is to place their child with a suitable family as soon as possible and so they will follow up approved families first. However, if you are within their geographical catchment area they may well decide to take up an application from you. This might be because you are the most suitable (or the only!) family who has responded to the child they featured. It might also be because they think that you are offering a valuable resource to a child, even if they cannot place that particular child with you.

The child's social worker might ask an agency local to you to do the assessment on their behalf, if you live at a distance. Alternatively, he or she might suggest that you contact a local agency, as there are other possibilities for the child whom they have featured. As discussed in Chapter 10, you need to think carefully about being assessed by an agency a long way away as it may be difficult for them to offer you adequate help and support once you have a child placed with you.

It felt a little surreal at first, looking at children's profiles on a website. So many children, all looking for a "forever family". We wondered if our future children would be among them. We found the video clips particularly helpful in trying to imagine what children's personalities were like. Reading the profiles made us more aware of some adoption-related issues and how we might prepare for them.

Adopters

What will happen after I've contacted an agency?

The process described below was introduced in England in 2013. There will be some variations in Wales and Northern Ireland, although the issues covered in preparation groups and in the assessment will be broadly the same.

1 Initial information gathering

Once you have contacted an adoption agency covering your area, they should respond within ten working days. They should invite you to an information meeting or offer you an individual visit or a pre-planned telephone call. These can take place in the evening or at a weekend if this suits you best. You will be given information on the adoption process and on the parenting needs of the children. This is an opportunity for you to consider whether adoption is likely to be right for you and how adopting a child who may have a range of complex needs will impact on your family. If you decide to proceed to the next stage, you need to complete a Registration of Interest form which the agency will supply. Among other things, this will authorise the agency to undertake the checks described in the next section. It will also confirm that you have not registered with any other agency. The agency should decide within five working days from receipt of your form whether or not to accept it. If the agency lacks the capacity to undertake assessments in the immediate future, it should advise you of this and offer to refer you to First4Adoption (see Useful Organisations) or to another agency.

2 Stage One – the pre-assessment process

This stage begins when the agency accepts your Registration of Interest and should normally take no more than two months to complete. The agency should discuss with you the work that will take place and should complete a written Stage One agreement with you detailing this. It should offer you some initial training and preparation and it must also complete the prescribed checks.

Checks are made of criminal records for you and members of your household aged over 18. Offences other than specified ones, i.e. those against children, need not rule you out, although the nature of the offence and how long ago it occurred will need to be carefully considered. It's vital that you are open and honest. Any attempt at deception will be taken very seriously. These checks are made to the

The adoption process (in England)

Adopters

Contacting agencies and expressing an interest

Information meeting(s)

Registration of Interest

Stage One – pre-assessment

Police, health and other checks

Personal referees contact

Some training and preparation

Stage Two – assessment

Further training and preparation

Work with an assessing social worker

Prospective Adopter's Report (PAR) completed

Adoption panel recommendation

Agency decision

Search for a child

Child

Statutory looked after child review

Adoption plan agreed

To adoption panel if parents agree to adoption

Agency decision on the adoption plan

To court if parents do not agree to adoption

Care order and placement order

Family finding

Matching meeting and report

Adoption panel recommendation

Agency decision

Placement planning meeting

Possible child appreciation day

Introductions

Placement

Review of placement

Adoption application

Adoption Order

Disclosure and Barring Service (DBS). Checks will also be made of the local authority where you live. You will be asked for the names of at least three personal referees, people who know you really well, and they will be interviewed. If you have parented children with a previous partner, the agency will want your permission to contact him or her. They may want to talk to adult children whom you've parented. They will want to check that you are not seriously in debt and that payments on your home are up to date. Finally, you will need a medical examination carried out by your GP. This will be considered by the adoption agency's medical adviser.

If the agency decides during or at the end of Stage One that you are not suitable to adopt, it must inform you in writing with clear reasons. You may make a complaint to the agency about this or raise concerns with First4Adoption. However, you are not able to apply to the Independent Review Mechanism. You may, if you wish, take a break of up to a maximum of six months after Stage One, or you may notify the agency that you wish to proceed straight to Stage Two.

3 Stage Two – the assessment process

I used my assessment to analyse what I really wanted and I thought hard about how much I value the size of my own family. I decided I actually wanted to adopt siblings!

Adopter

This stage starts when the agency receives notification from you that you wish to proceed with the assessment process. It finishes with the agency decision about your suitability as an adopter and should normally be completed within four months. A Stage Two written assessment plan must be completed with you, detailing the assessment process, dates for meetings and agreed training. The social worker designated to work with you will visit you at your home. The purpose of these visits is for the social worker to gain a detailed view of you and other family members in the home, in order to assess your suitability to adopt a child.

Some of the issues that will be covered with you will be:

- your life history, and experiences of being parented;
- your relationships, past and present, with wider family, friends and partners;
- your personality and interests;
- your ethnicity, culture and religion;
- your reasons for wanting to adopt and your expectations;
- your parenting experience and skills;
- your openness towards birth families;
- your support network, using support and problem-solving skills;
- employment and finance;
- strengths and limitations.

The social worker will want to talk with any children you may already have, both those at home and usually with adult children living elsewhere. They will usually also want to meet an ex-partner with whom you have parented children. They may well want to talk further with your referees, although they will have had contact with them during Stage One of the process.

All adoption agencies are required to provide preparation and training and you will almost certainly be invited to a series of group meetings, often about six, of two to three hours each. You will be with other prospective adopters, usually about eight or ten people. As well as hearing from social workers about adoption and the children waiting, you will usually also hear from experienced adopters, an adopted adult and perhaps from a birth parent whose child has been adopted, about their experiences. You will have the opportunity to ask questions and to reflect on your own life experiences and on the impact of any adopted child on your family and how you will adapt to meet their needs.

I sat in the car park for ages, trying to pluck up the courage to get out of the car. I don't know what I was scared of. Not *being good enough, I suppose. Once I got in it was fine. Everyone was welcoming and they were a very diverse group of people. I had thought it would be all couples, all white, but there was a real mixture.*

Adopter, *Looking after our Own*

The issues covered will include:

- why children need to be adopted;
- issues of loss, separation and trauma;
- how children become attached to their carers and the effect on them of the poor attachments that they are likely to have experienced;
- the significance of continuity and contact for children who are separated from their birth family;
- the sorts of behaviour that children who have been neglected and abused may display;
- the key parenting skills that are likely to be needed;
- support networks and support services.

I found the training really informative. I know some people thought there was too much focus on negative things, but I didn't want the agency painting a glossy picture and then a child going back into care because I couldn't cope.

Adopter

What exactly are they looking for?

Social workers are looking for people who:

- can make and keep close relationships;
- are open and honest, able to talk about their feelings and about their limitations as well as their strengths;
- are adaptable, flexible and willing and able to resolve and learn

from difficult experiences;

- enjoy children and are willing and able to put the child's needs first;
- know that every child, even a tiny baby, comes with a past and a birth family who are important;
- have "staying power" and a sense of humour.

Although this process is thorough, searching and quite intrusive, many prospective adopters actually quite like the opportunity to reflect on their life and on their relationships and find it a stimulating and interesting experience. Often, a good and trusting relationship is built up with the social worker.

It was good to talk about our plans for the future and to reflect on the past. You quite often forget the good things that have happened in the past but I remembered friendships I formed as a child and how I used to play. It helped me to get into the framework of looking at things from a child's perspective.

Adopter, *The Pink Guide to Adoption*

What can I do if I have concerns at this stage?

If you are concerned that adoption, at this point in your life, may not be right for you, you should discuss this with your social worker. You can, of course, withdraw from the process at any point. It is much better to be open about any doubts or concerns that you have at this stage rather than waiting until you are linked with a child.

You may still be keen on adoption but, as happens occasionally, be finding it difficult to work with your social worker. You need to try to share your concerns with your worker but if you can't resolve things between you, you could consider contacting their manager for help. It is possible, although quite unusual, to have a change of worker part-way through the process.

You can, of course, withdraw your application from that agency at any point. However, if you apply elsewhere you may well have to start again from the beginning. The second agency will also need to contact the first one for any comments that they may have. You should be able to see anything that is put in writing (provided it doesn't include third party information, for example, from your referees).

Fast-track approval process

This is available to anyone who is an approved foster carer in England and to people who have previously adopted in a court in England or Wales under the Adoption Agencies Regulations 2005 (or Welsh equivalent). If this applies to you, you will be able to enter the adoption approval process at Stage Two. Agencies are required to complete the process within four months.

The assessment report

A written report will be compiled, with your help. You must be given a copy of the report to read, apart from the medical information, checks and information from your personal referees (which remain confidential to the agency). You have five working days under English regulations in which to comment, in writing if necessary, on anything that you disagree with the social worker about or that you think should be added. CoramBAAF's Prospective Adopter's Report (PAR) (England) is widely used by agencies in England.

The whole home study business is like opening a Pandora's box and this person takes you on a journey through issues you've never analysed before. Unless you feel safe with the social worker, it could be tempting to cover things up.

Adopter

The adoption panel

The report is presented to the agency's adoption panel for their recommendation. This is a group of up to about 10 people, including social work professionals, a medical adviser, and independent members, who are people with knowledge of and an interest in adoption. These almost always include at least one adoptive parent and an adopted adult. Adoption panels are there to consider prospective adopters and to make a recommendation to the agency about whether they are suitable to adopt or not.

You must be invited to attend the panel, or at least part of it, if you wish. The majority of prospective adopters do attend. Most are very nervous beforehand but find the actual experience less daunting than they thought. Panel members find it extremely helpful to meet prospective adopters and to have the opportunity to have a brief discussion with them.

The panel may consider and give advice to the agency about the number, age range, sex, likely needs and background of children whom you could adopt. However, it is the agency which makes the final decision on this.

Occasionally the panel will defer making a recommendation, pending additional work being done or information gathered. You will need to clarify exactly what is being asked for and by when.

The final decision

After the panel has made its recommendation, a senior officer in the agency considers whether or not to approve you as an adopter. In England and Wales, if the agency is proposing not to approve you, they must write to you first giving you their reasons and asking for your comments. In England, applicants at this stage have 40 working days within which to make comments (representations), either to the decision maker or to the Independent Review Mechanism (IRM) (see below), but not to both. In Wales, applicants have 40 working days to apply to the Independent Review Mechanism Cymru (see below). In England and Wales, the agency must write and tell you their final decision, whether it is approval or non-approval. It should be unlikely for you to get to this stage and not be aware of any concerns about you from your social worker. The vast majority of people who get to this stage in the process are approved as adopters.

A month later we had our panel again, this time for real. We were well prepared and knew who would be on the panel, but it was still unnerving when we walked through the door and saw all these faces staring at us. The panel members went over all of the issues that had come up during our assessment and asked some quite unexpected questions, which we dealt with OK. Then, feeling a mixture of excitement and trepidation, we went back home to wait. When we got the call to say we had been approved we were unbelievably excited and thought 'That's it, we're going to have children at last!'

Adopters

A brief report

Occasionally social workers will decide, before they have completed the assessment, that they will not be able to recommend you as suitable to adopt. They will discuss their concerns with you and you will have the option of withdrawing from the process. However, if you decide that you want to proceed, the social workers can write a brief report which, in England, is then treated in the same way as a full report, i.e. you must see it and can comment on it, it will go to the panel and then to the decision maker. If the decision maker proposes not to approve you, you will have the right to apply to the

IRM in England or Wales (provided that your agency is in one of these countries).

Independent Review Mechanism (IRM) England

This is run by Coram Children's Legal Centre on behalf of the Department for Education. It is only available to people assessed by adoption agencies in England. If you receive written notification from the agency, following a panel, that it proposes not to approve you (or to terminate your approval), you can apply to the IRM. You must do this within 40 working days. The IRM will arrange for your case to be heard by an independent IRM panel, which you can attend. The IRM panel will make a recommendation which will go to your agency. The agency decision maker will then make the final decision.

Independent Review Mechanism Cymru

This is run by Children in Wales on behalf of the Welsh Assembly and is available to people assessed by adoption agencies in Wales. It operates in a very similar way to the IRM in England.

What happens if I'm not approved?

If the agency has not been able to approve you, you should discuss with them fully the reasons why. They will have been disappointed not to be able to approve you and will have thought about this very carefully and so you may agree with them that perhaps adoption is not for you. However, you can, if you wish, approach other adoption agencies and start again. Sometimes, people turned down by one agency are approved by another and go on to adopt successfully.

If you feel that the service that you have had from the agency has been poor you can, if you wish, make a formal complaint about this to the agency.

Do I have to pay the agency?

There is no charge for the home study, assessment and preparation if you are adopting a child who is in the UK. However, if you are asking an agency to do a home study so you can adopt a child from abroad, they will probably make a charge (see Chapter 7).

How long will it all take?

This process, from your Registration of Interest to approval by the agency, should not usually take more than six months. This is the timescale in the Guidance to the Adoption and Children Act for England.

However, the Guidance does recognise that there may be "exceptional circumstances" that mean that the agency needs to take longer or, of course, you may want or need to take longer. You may want more time to think things over or to prepare your children or other family members or there may be events in your life which mean you need to take a short break. You should talk this over with your social worker.

4

How do I find a child?

The matching process – I am beginning to understand that this is what they've really been preparing us for all this time. It's difficult, it's emotional and it feels like it's never going to end. Every day that passes, we are desperate to hear about another lead, another child who may become part of our lives forever. And we've been lucky. There have been leads – several of them. [Our social worker] has mentioned three or four possibilities and we have even attended an Adoption Exchange Day run by a consortium of local authorities, where you swap flyers advertising yourselves with details of children looking for a family.

It's not as if we have been short of possible matches. Unfortunately, each time we have heard about one, something has come up that rules them out for us.

[But one day], Lesley doesn't say a word when I walk through our front door. She simply hands me a piece of paper she has collected in person from the children's services office this afternoon. I look down and realise I have a flyer in my hands with a picture and short description of a beautiful baby boy.

Mike, adoptive dad, *Frozen*

What happens after approval?

Once you have been approved as suitable to adopt a child, the agency must prepare a written matching agreement with you, setting out the matching process and your role in identifying a possible child for placement with you.

If you have been approved by a local authority, they will consider you carefully for their waiting children or for a child from the local consortium of agencies to which they may belong. Unless a link with a specific child is being considered, the local authority must, with your agreement and within three months, refer you to the Adoption Register for England or the Wales Adoption Register for active consideration for children referred to the Register, or to the Adoption Regional Information System (ARIS) if you are in Northern Ireland.

If you have been approved by a voluntary adoption agency, they will help you to find a waiting child. They will encourage you to use family-finding services such as Children who Wait (run by Adoption UK) or Link Maker, and they will probably agree to refer you to your country's Adoption Register or ARIS straight away. (See Useful Organisations for more information.)

Adoption Registers also organise Adoption Exchange Days which approved adopters can attend by invitation. A number of adoption agencies generally attend the events with details of children needing adopting (generally those who have been waiting longer). Social workers will be available to answer questions and provide more information about the children. Your agency should be able to give you information about events in your area.

Some local authorities and voluntary adoption agencies organise Adoption Activity Days, which are a way for prospective adopters who are approved or nearly approved to get to meet some of the children who are waiting for a family. Adopters and children have the opportunity to interact over fun activities like face painting, cake decorating and soft play. A lot of careful organisation and preparation go into these events so that children can focus on having fun. Support is available for prospective adopters if they feel overwhelmed at the event. Children's social workers and foster carers are available for chats, and adopters can also invite their social worker for support. Your agency should be able to give you information about any Adoption Activity Days you can attend.

When we first embarked on this journey of approval, the panel was the major event we were working towards. However, the highs of panel approval are short-lived, with the feelings being replaced with "when will we be matched?"

Adopter

Considering possible children

To this day, we still don't know what attracted us to their profile. There wasn't very much information, and no photo. Just a picture of two teddy bears! [When we saw their photos two months later] Chantelle looked very much how I imagined her to be, though Evie was a little different from the picture I had in my head. But both James and I thought, 'They're our girls. Now the picture is complete.'

Adopters of two girls

Your agency may approach you to discuss a possible child or you may respond to a child whom you see featured as needing a new family. You will probably talk with your own social worker first and with the child's social worker. You will also be given written information about the child and possibly see a short video of them. You will then meet the child's social worker and also, perhaps, their foster carer. It is important, in the excitement of hearing about a possible child at last, that you take time to consider the child's needs carefully and how you will be able to meet them. You may want to follow up particular issues with the social workers, the foster carers or a doctor, or check whether the necessary services, for example, special schooling, are available in your area. It is important that you have as much information as possible about the child and their background. Your social worker has a responsibility to ensure that you receive this and should help you consider it.

It is a learning process and we are working out how to filter the information more efficiently. It is hard to reject children but you have to be realistic, you have to weigh up what the child needs and what you can offer.

Adopter, *The Pink Guide to Adoption*

The child's social workers may still be considering other families at this stage. They should keep you and your social worker in touch with what is happening. If they decide that another family has more to offer this particular child, they should try to explain this to you.

Fostering for Adoption (FfA)

Fostering for Adoption enables children – usually young children – to be placed with carers who may become their adopters. The process was designed to help more children live with permanent families as soon as possible after leaving their birth family and to avoid them being moved from carer to carer too often. This involves agencies giving an approved adopter temporary approval as a foster carer for a named child. The child can therefore be placed as a foster child with carers without them having had a full fostering assessment or panel approval as foster carers. The terminology "Fostering for Adoption" applies to England only but in Scotland, Northern Ireland and Wales, placements may also start on a fostering basis.

Placing children with carers who may become their adopters avoids the damage caused by ending temporary foster carer relationships which children will have experienced as their primary parenting relationship. It also allows children to experience security and stability during the essential time of their early months and years. All these advantages will apply for the children's carers/adopters as well.

Local authorities will only seek Fostering for Adoption placements when it is clear that the child's birth parents are unlikely to resolve the issues that led to the child being taken into care, and that no other members of the birth family can take care of the child. Although it is highly likely that these children will be adopted at a later stage, no plan for adoption exists at this initial stage. The child will be fostered until, in most cases, work with birth parents and court involvement enables an adoption plan to be agreed and the child to be matched for adoption with these carers at panel. However, there is a risk that, for some reason, adoption will not be agreed as the plan or court involvement will take longer than anticipated, and carers will need to be prepared for this eventuality and any feelings of disappointment and loss if the child is not placed with them permanently.

If you might be interested in becoming an FfA carer, you should discuss this with your agency during your assessment. There is a useful free leaflet available about becoming a carer through Fostering for Adoption – visit www.coram.org.uk/resource/fostering-adoption-leaflet-carers.

Concurrent planning

Concurrent planning is a way of finding permanent families for babies and children under two who have been removed from their family, and who may either be adopted, or go back to their parents.

See Chapter 8 for more details.

Being matched with a child

The Adoption Agencies Regulations for England introduce fairly detailed requirements for this part of the process. Arrangements in other parts of the UK will be broadly similar but not identical – your social worker can give you more information.

Once the child's social worker has decided that you seem to be the right family for a particular child and you are also keen to proceed, they must give you a copy of the child's permanence report (a comprehensive report about the child, comparable to your assessment form). They must also give you any other reports and information on the child's health, education or special needs that would be helpful. They should meet with you to discuss all this, including the plans for any post-placement contact for the child with birth relatives or others. If you and they are keen to proceed, they should then assess what adoption support you and the child will need.

The social worker should then write an adoption placement report which should include the proposed contact and support arrangements. You must be given 10 days to read and comment on this.

This report, plus your assessment form and the child's permanence report, will be presented to an adoption panel, usually the one in the child's local authority. Your social worker and the child's social worker will attend and you will also be invited to attend. It can be extremely helpful to the panel if you can do so.

Similarly to the approval process, it is a senior officer in the local authority who makes the decision about the match, based on the recommendation of the panel.

It is unusual that matches are not agreed at this stage, although it can happen. Occasionally recommendations and decisions are deferred if the panel or agency requires more information. There is no formal appeal process if a match is turned down.

What support and help will be available?

It is very important that you discuss with both the child's social worker and your social worker at this matching stage, what sort of support and help you and the child will need after placement. As described above, there should be a written plan, discussed and agreed with you, about this. It should cover any special arrangements that need to be made to meet the child's educational and health needs and any therapy that may be needed. It should also cover the support and help that will be available to you. If you will need financial help, the necessary means test should be done and an agreement made as to the level and frequency of any payments.

One adoptive parent, if in employment, is entitled to statutory adoption leave for one year. The Statutory Adoption Pay rate is approximately £140 at the time of writing, or 90 per cent of average weekly earnings, whichever is the lower, and is paid for the first 39 weeks. The other parent, if there are two, if employed, is entitled to two weeks' statutory leave at the same rate. To qualify for either, you must have completed 26 weeks of continuous service with your employer up to the date of matching.

For more details on help and support available when a child has been placed with you, see Chapter 5.

What is a child appreciation day?

Some, but not all, agencies arrange these days. They invite all the key people who have known the child, such as former foster carers, teachers and relatives, to meet with you. This enables you to build up a really detailed and "living" picture of the child and their life so far.

I think you're so nervous about meeting the people because you know they've chosen you because they think you're better. I mean, they've looked through a whole catalogue or magazine…and seen you and thought that's who they wanted. So you feel nervous about meeting them. You think, 'Well, am I going to be good enough?'

Adopted girl, *Adopted Children Speaking*

Introductions and moving in

Once a decision has been made about a match, the social workers will meet with you to confirm plans for support, for contact with the birth family, for your exercise of your parental responsibility and for introductions with the child. They will work out with you and with the child's foster carers a plan for introducing you and the child to each other. Introductions with the child may be daily for a week for a young baby, or more spaced out over a longer period for an older child – although they do not usually last more than six to eight weeks.

Many adopters prepare a little book for the child with photos of themselves, their pets, their house, etc, and some prepare a short film. These are then shared with the child by their foster carers prior to the first meeting. Most foster carers are skilled at preparing and supporting children to move on, although it is an emotional time for them, as well as for you and the child.

You should discuss any doubts or concerns that you may have with the social workers during this period. If you really do not feel that the match is right, it is much better to say so at this stage rather than later.

I can't begin to tell you how wonderful it was to welcome our daughter home. We had put together an album that the foster carers read to our daughter every night before she met us, with a picture of her "forever" mummy and daddy, her bedroom, her garden and her new dog! This helped prepare her, and resulted in her first words to us when we met her, which were 'Hello Mummy'. We will never forget that moment.

Adopters

_____

5

What happens after a child moves in?

There is so much pressure for adoption to be perfect…it was a shock for us to discover that not every moment was idyllic…While being thrilled and feeling privileged to be a family, we also had to face the reality of changing nappies and having food sprayed all over the walls. But we soon came to see that the ups and downs of adoption were simply the ups and downs of being a family.

Has it all lived up to the dream? Well, the dream didn't bother to mention the tantrums, the tears, the exhaustion or any illness. But nor did it prepare us for the depth of feeling we would have for our little precious girls. It's noisier, and definitely smellier, than I'd imagined. But the reality is also funnier, and more amazing, and nothing is taken for granted in the daily routine. We just look forward to every day of having them with us.

Laurel and David, adopters of two sisters, both aged under two, *Take Two*

Your child or children moving in is only the beginning. Adjusting to a different way of life will take time and there will be difficult periods. You and your child may well need help and it is important that you speak to your social worker about any concerns. Asking for help isn't a sign of weakness, but shows that you are being proactive and willing to address difficulties.

Parental responsibility

The Adoption and Children Act 2002 gives adoptive parents in England and Wales parental responsibility on placement, rather than just on adoption, as formerly. You will share this with the child's birth parents and with the local authority that is placing the child with you. The local authority must discuss with you, before they place the child, whether they propose to restrict your exercise of your parental responsibility in any way. You could agree, for instance, that they will still be involved in decisions about visits abroad or health treatment. Once the child is adopted, you have exclusive parental responsibility with no restrictions.

What help will be available?

As described in the previous chapter, it is important to talk to your social worker and to the child's social worker, before the child moves in, about the help, support and special services that may be necessary. You should, if you are adopting in England, have a written Adoption Placement Plan, that has been discussed and agreed with you. This should cover support arrangements as well as arrangements for contact with the birth family, and for the exercise of your parental responsibility. If appropriate, referrals should already have been made for specialist therapy or educational or health services that your child may need. This will be especially important if you are adopting an older child who may have experienced considerable trauma, or a child who has suffered from neglect or abuse. In such cases, access to appropriate help will be crucial.

Social workers from the adoption agency that assessed and approved you, as well as from the child's agency, if different, will offer you all the help they can during the settling-in period. They are required to visit at regular intervals and to review how things are going. Adoption UK also offers invaluable support and help to adoptive families, and there are local groups throughout the UK.

When [my adoptive son] first moved in I found it so difficult, and now I look back and I'm astonished at how hard I found it 'cause now, it's not always easy – I used to think I was very tolerant and patient and I'm not, I'm intolerant and very impatient [laughs], which is a bit sad 'cause it can affect your view of yourself, but I think we've got a very good relationship.

Adoptive mum, *Gay, Lesbian and Heterosexual Adoptive Families*

Will there be any financial help?

You should be clear before the child moves in about any practical and financial support available. Many local authorities pay a settling-in grant, especially if you are adopting older children, which could be several hundred pounds, to cover your initial outlay on equipment such as beds and car seats. If you are adopting a group of brothers and sisters, it is possible for them to pay towards, for example, a larger car and for equipment such as a large washing machine. Regular financial support – an adoption allowance – may be available for certain children – a group of brothers and sisters, for example, or a child with disabilities or serious behavioural difficulties. This regular financial support is means tested but you should enquire about this if you think you need this help at any stage. There is an annual paper review of your means, which determines the level of any financial support.

---

*You need to consider how much time and energy you have –
and will have. Like any parent, you need to make some
adjustments. It's helpful to have lots of support. Check what
childcare is on offer in your area. Try to seek the support of
your employers.*

Adopters

Will support be available after adoption?

Many adoption agencies have "after adoption" or "post-adoption"
workers. They keep in touch with families who have adopted
through the agency and offer the opportunity to talk over issues.
They also often organise group events for adopters on subjects such
as managing difficult behaviour or talking to children about
adoption. They can also help you access specialist services that you
and your child may need. There are also After Adoption or Post-
Adoption Centres, which exist to help families. Adoption UK can also
provide valuable support from other experienced adopters.

---

*I couldn't have done it without any of them. Some have been
"all-rounders", while I've put others into categories; for
instance, the person who is brilliant with practical support but
brushes emotional things under the carpet. But every single
person has played a part in helping me.*

Adopters

Having your support needs assessed

Adoption Support Services Regulations for England make it clear that adoptive families have the right to request and be given an assessment of their adoption support needs, including the need for financial help, at any stage in the child's childhood. The responsibility for this assessment stays with the local authority that placed the child for three years after the Adoption Order. After this, the responsibility for the assessment moves to the local authority in which you live. There are also published policies in relation to adoption support for Northern Ireland.

First4Adoption, on behalf of the Department for Education, has put together a practical guide to post-adoption support available in England for adopters and their children, called the Adoption Passport. It is available from their website at: www.first4adoption.org.uk/adoption-support/.

The Adoption Support Fund (ASF)

Adopters in England can access the Adoption Support Fund (ASF), which was established to help families access funds for therapeutic support.

The ASF is available for children living in England up to and including the age of 21 (or 25 with a Statement of Special Educational Needs or Education Health & Care Plan) who:

- are adopted and were previously in local authority care in England, Wales, Scotland and Northern Ireland;
- are adopted from overseas;
- are subject to a Special Guardianship Order.

To access the ASF, your family's adoption support needs will have to be assessed by the local authority. The ASF will provide money for a range of therapeutic services if it is shown that they can help achieve one of the following positive outcomes for you and your child:

- improved relationships with friends, family members, teachers and school staff;

- improved engagement with learning;
- improved emotional regulation and behaviour management;
- improved confidence and ability to enjoy a positive family life and social relationships.

You can read more about the Adoption Support Fund on the First4Adoption website: www.first4adoption.org.uk/adoption-support/adoption-support-fund. CoramBAAF also publishes a guide for parents, *The Adopter's Handbook on Therapy*, that provides information on a range of different therapies and how they may be able to help children (see Useful Reading).

What about the birth family?

Birth parents whose children are adopted usually find this a hard and painful experience. Occasionally they have requested adoption, but usually the decision has been made by others, sometimes much against their own wishes. However, they are often still important to their children and many of them are prepared to co-operate with the adopters and the agency in offering what they can to their child.

It is usually to the benefit of the child if the adopters can meet the birth parents at least once and continue to exchange basic information about the child. This is usually through the adoption agency which acts as a "letterbox" for a letter, perhaps once a year. This is known as "indirect" or "letterbox" contact. It is now recognised that maintaining some level of contact can be of benefit to children as they grow up and helps the adopters answer questions about the birth parents, what they were like, where they are now, and so on. Ongoing contact will not be right in all cases and will need to be handled sensitively.

I think it's important, I think it will be important to him as an adult. I don't think it's important to him now particularly. I think in a way he'd prefer not to think about it or not to talk about it…but I understand its purpose and I think when he's older he will appreciate those letters.

Adoptive dad, *Gay, Lesbian and Heterosexual Adoptive Families*

For some children, visits may continue after adoption. This may be with birth parents or with grandparents and other significant adults, or it may be with brothers and sisters who are living elsewhere, perhaps in other adoptive families. Older children may know where their relatives are living and want a family who can help them keep in contact. Again, this is something that you, the agency, and the child, if old enough, will need to discuss and agree on well before the adoption goes through to court. However, it is important to remember that the child's needs and wishes will change over time and you do need to be prepared to be flexible.

We have annual letterbox contact with our son's birth mother. It's hard work building up to it – I wonder each time what to say, how his birth mother will picture him from the letter and photos…It tears me to shreds, writing a letter once a year. There's a huge sense of relief afterwards. But at the same time I feel overwhelming love for him. It doesn't upset me to send the letter, but brings me that feeling of love.

Adoptive mum, *Could you be my Parent?*

Why do children have to know they are adopted?

Many children who are adopted were old enough when placed to remember something of their past and so they obviously know about their adoption. However, all children have the right to know about their past. Increasingly, it has been acknowledged that an open rather than a secretive attitude is more helpful to the child. After all, there is always the danger that someone else will tell the child without any warning, or perhaps in a hostile way, for example, in a family row. Finding out like this can be a terrible shock to a child who may well wonder what else you have concealed from them.

Even older children may be very confused about what happened in the past. They may blame themselves for the things that went wrong in their birth family. So it is important to be honest and to discuss adoption quite naturally, right from the start.

From the age of 18 in England, Wales and Northern Ireland, adopted children have the right to their original birth certificate if they want it – although their adoptive parents may already have given it to them.

The CoramBAAF book, *Talking about Adoption to your Adopted Child*, can help you with the kind of issues you will face (see Useful Reading). This is when the information collected by the adoption agency about the child's birth parents and early life, often in a life story book, will be needed. Children who are not given any facts sometimes have fantasies about their circumstances or history and may well believe the worst, so it is kinder and fairer to tell them the truth. This is not something that you can do just once. Children need to go over their story again at different stages in their growing up, understanding a bit more each time.

You go through a phase of reading his life story book, like, most evenings for maybe a week or so, and then nothing again for another month or six weeks or something like that.

Adoptive mum, *Gay, Lesbian and Heterosexual Adoptive Families*

Social networking websites and contact

Social networking websites such as Facebook have had a huge impact on the way that people communicate with each other.

Finding and contacting people is much easier than ever before, with both positive and negative outcomes.

It is important that you are aware of the way in which the use of the internet, social media and the widespread use of smartphones are changing the whole context of adoption contact. You need to know what you can do to protect privacy and security in the best interests of your child. However, you also need to recognise that there is a limit to how far you can control and monitor the use of these forms of contact by your child and/or members of their birth family. You may need to manage complex situations which arise from unauthorised and unmediated contact. CoramBAAF publishes a guide for parents, *Facing up to Facebook*, that explores these issues.

What if the adoption doesn't work out?

Some adoptions do go wrong – like marriages, they do not always work. The first few weeks and months can produce problems that no one anticipated so there is always a settling-in period of at least three months, and usually considerably longer, before an Adoption Order is made. Of course, the social worker from the agency will keep in touch with you and will help and support you as much as possible. If you feel that things really are going wrong during this period, and that you cannot continue with the adoption, you owe it to yourself and to the child to tell the agency.

Once the adoption has been made legal, the child will be legally yours just as if you had given birth to him or her. The sources of help described above will be available. If the problems cannot be resolved, the local authority can take responsibility for the child again. However, the adoptive parents will remain the child's legal parents until and unless the child is adopted again by new parents.

A large-scale study on adoption disruptions, published in 2014 (*Beyond the Adoption Order*, available from CoramBAAF), estimated that nine per cent of adoptive placements come to an end before the child reaches 18. The child's age at placement is one of the major factors, with the risk increasing the older the child is at placement: adoption placements are ten times more likely to break down in the teenage years, compared with children under the age of four.

Adoptive families should be trusted and treated as responsible parents unless there are concerns about safeguarding the children. Above all else, when adoptive families are in a state of crisis, they must be taken seriously! Their views need to be heard, their perceptions have to be taken into account and their pain has to be acknowledged.

Karen, adoptive mum, *Adoption Undone*

What will happen to the child if things don't work out?

If the child does have to leave, he or she will go either to a foster family or possibly to a residential home. If it isn't possible to resolve the difficulties with you, another adoptive home may be found, but the difficulties that arose between you and the child will have to be understood to try and prevent the same thing happening again. Usually, agencies arrange a meeting, called a disruption meeting, that enables everyone concerned to come together and reflect on events and what can be learned from them. Sometimes the problems arise when the child is much older, and, like many teenagers, is having difficulty feeling at home in a family setting. The best solution then may be to support the child in an "independent" setting such as lodgings. He or she may well value having you around to advise and reassure him or her even if living together is too difficult at that point in their lives.

Things are very good for my daughter…we have put a lot of work into supporting her and trying to draw her back into the family after some nightmare years…so far, so good…and we love her to smithereens…that's all we have left after being brought very low over a long period of time…the love.

Adoptive mum, *Facing up to Facebook*

Could I try again?

You may feel that you and the child were not right for one another, and that things could work out better with a different child. If the social worker agrees with you, you may get the chance to adopt again. After all, different children need different families and just as a second attempt may work for a child, so it may work for a family. You could apply to the same agency again or to a different one. You would need a further period of assessment and preparation and the adoption panel and the agency would need to consider whether or not to approve you again to adopt.

6

How is adoption made legal?

Peter is very excited while having his breakfast and cannot wait to get all dressed up to see the judge. When the taxi arrives to take us to the court, it is an amazing feeling, knowing that within the hour Peter will legally be our son…

The judge is a very pleasant woman and she immediately gives Peter a party bag full of balloons and sweets. Typically, he shoves a brightly coloured lollipop into his mouth straight away – so that for the entire rest of the hearing he can barely utter a word.

The judge then asks Rob and me a few questions about our life with Peter, and she wants to know how he is settling in at nursery.

After five more minutes of chat and looking at photos, the judge officially signs the adoption order. Then our adoption hearing is over. Clare leans towards us and says, 'He's yours!'

I simply want to cry.

Maria, adoptive mum, *An Adoption Diary*

When you adopt a child, you become the child's legal parent. The child usually takes your surname and can inherit from you just as if he or she was born to you. All responsibility for making decisions about the child and his or her future is transferred to the adopters.

An adoption is not legal without an Adoption Order made by a court. Once an Order has been made, it is irrevocable and cannot be overturned.

I love reading the ending of a book because of the feeling of triumph that you've finished it…and I guess that was the same feeling in court, watching them close the book, really shutting it…Knowing that nothing else was going to happen. It was just going to be an ordinary life from now on.

Adopted girl, *Adopted Children Speaking*

How do I get an Adoption Order?

You have to apply to court for an Adoption Order. You apply in England and Wales to your local Magistrates' Family Proceedings Court, to a County Court that deals with adoption (now a network of designated adoption centres), or to the High Court; in Northern Ireland you apply to the County Court or to the High Court. Your adoption agency should be able to help you with the process and the court. You will need to obtain an application form from the court and complete and return it. If you are not adopting a child who is looked after by a local authority, you will also need to notify the children's services in your area of your intention to adopt at least three months before you apply to court. They will have a duty to visit you and your child and to prepare a report for the court.

When can I apply to court?

The Adoption and Children Act for England and Wales requires that if your child has been placed with you by an adoption agency, he or she must have lived with you in the 10 weeks before you make the application to court. If your child is older or has special needs, you will probably want to wait longer and give yourselves a chance to settle down together properly before applying to court. You will need to discuss with your social worker when the right time would be to apply to court. There are different timescales for relatives, step-parents and others adopting a child who has not been looked after and placed by an adoption agency. These are detailed in the relevant chapters. In Northern Ireland, the child must have lived with you for at least 13 weeks before an Adoption Order can be made, if placed by an adoption agency.

What happens before the court hearing?

Before the court can consider your application, it will require a social worker from the local authority that placed your child with you, or from the one where you live if your child was not placed by a local authority, to prepare a report. It is a detailed report that includes information about your child and their birth family, about you and about the placement, both the reasons for it and also how it is going. In England and Wales, a Children's Guardian may be asked by the court to prepare a report in some cases. These workers will need to talk with you and your child, as well as with the birth parents.

What happens in court?

Adoption hearings are usually very short if the child's birth parents are in agreement. You need not expect it to last more than half an hour, and you should be told at once whether the Adoption Order is granted. A report will have been prepared for the court that the Judge or Magistrates will consider. You will probably be asked some questions, and so will the child, if he or she is old enough. The Judge must consider the views of the child, taking account of the child's age and understanding. The only reason to dispense or do away with the child's consent is if he or she is incapable of consenting. Many courts try to make the occasion as relaxed and celebratory as possible.

The judge asked my mum and dad if they wanted to adopt me and my brother. They replied, 'Yes, we do'…Then she asked me. I felt nervous but I said I wanted to stay with my new family. She asked Anthony what he wanted to do and he said stay. Then the judge said, 'I will write in my book that today Anthony and James became members of the Smith family'.

James, age 11, *The Colours in Me*

What if the birth parents don't agree?

In England and Wales, a local authority must have authorisation to place a child with you before it can do so. This authorisation is either formal, signed consent by the child's birth parent(s) or it is a court order, called a Placement Order. Once this authorisation has been given and the child has been placed with you and you have applied to court, it will only be in exceptional cases that the birth parents will be able to contest the adoption and they will need the leave of the court to do this.

In non-agency placements in England and Wales, if the birth parents do not agree, the adopters have to ask the court to override their wishes. The court can only do this in appropriate circumstances, for instance, if it judges that the parents are unreasonably refusing to agree. Cases like this are known as contested adoptions and if you are involved in one you will almost certainly need legal help. You should be able to obtain help with the costs, either through public funding (formerly legal aid) or from the adoption agency, and it is worth finding out about this at an early stage.

Are there any other legal issues?

Yes, a few, but if, as is likely, you are adopting through an adoption agency, it will usually sort things out for you. You can only receive a child for adoption in this country if he or she is placed by a UK adoption agency or via the High Court, unless the child is a close relative. Remember that any other private arrangement to adopt is illegal.

Three years later and here we are settled together as a family! I have my nightmare days, heartaches, fears and frustrations, but then the children will come out with something really funny, and all is well again! I take the rough with the smooth.

Adopter

Will my child get a new "birth certificate" when he or she is adopted?

Yes, your child will be issued with a new short certificate in your name which looks the same as other short birth certificates. If you wish, you can apply for a long "birth" certificate, which will give your names and your child's new name. It will have "Copy of an entry in the adoption register" printed on it.

What about legal fees?

If the birth parents do not agree to the adoption and decide to oppose it in court, it may get so complicated that you need a solicitor and a barrister. This means legal costs can rise, in some cases, to several thousand pounds. But you may be able to claim public funding – it depends on your income – or the local authority responsible for the child will usually pay most, or all, of the legal costs involved.

There is a fee for the court application but many local authorities will pay this when you are adopting a child for whom they are responsible.

_____

Being adopted means that when I grow up and have kids, my Dad and Pop can look after them.

Boy of six adopted by a gay male couple, *Proud Parents*
_____

7

What about adoption from abroad?

There are still many unanswered questions in my mind: How can I help our children to be happy? How can I help them to appreciate being part of a multiracial family? How will our family experience adoption in the future?...I want to make sure that I find a way to ensure that our children's loss and the events of their early lives are not minimised. I have to let them know that I accept that their beginnings, marked by relinquishment, separation and loss, will forever be with them...

At the same time it is not fair to cocoon them. When they go out into society on their own, as they are increasingly doing, they need to be fully equipped to navigate our racially changed world. But issues of "race" or other prejudice are not the only concerns. Too much emphasis on the specific aspects of our children's heritage and history will blind us to the wider task of being parents.

Stevan, adoptive dad of two children adopted from overseas, *Finding our Familia*

Some families are moved by the plight of children who have been the victims of war or natural disaster, or who have been abandoned in orphanages, and come forward to offer them a home. Others, who may not be able to adopt the child whom they feel able or want to parent in the UK, may also seek to adopt from another country. In some cases, families may want to adopt a child who is a relative and lives in another country.

Where can I get advice before deciding on this?

You can approach your local authority. There is also a helpline run by the Department for Education and another run independently by the Intercountry Adoption Centre, and Adoption UK can discuss adoption generally. Written information is available from all these agencies and from CoramBAAF (see Useful Organisations and Useful Reading). Many of the issues that you will need to consider are also relevant to UK adoption and are covered in Chapter 2.

Surely adoption overseas is the best plan for children living in extreme poverty?

It may be the best plan for some children in the short term. However, children have the right to remain in their own community and their own country, if at all possible, and countries overseas are working to this end. They need help from more affluent countries, and from individuals in those countries, to achieve this. In some countries, the "loss" of their children to overseas adoption has triggered the development of adoption services, and programmes to improve child care services have been launched, sometimes in collaboration with or funded by child care services from more "developed" countries.

The numbers of adoptions from overseas has declined slightly and is in the region of 100–150 per year. One of the reasons for this decline is that more countries overseas are developing their own adoption services.

Wouldn't countries in crisis welcome this sort of help?

In an emergency, it is impossible to gather the information needed to make a decision about whether the child really needs adoption. For example, are the child's parents alive or not? They may be in hospital, in prison, in hiding or refugees in another country, and may re-emerge to claim their child later. Intercountry adoption is not a suitable way of dealing with the needs of children who are moved as a result of war, famine, or other emergency. Indeed, many of these children will be emotionally damaged by abandonment, malnutrition, the effects of war, and family separation. In a crisis, the child needs to be made safe in as familiar an environment as possible. Experienced aid workers find that the vast majority of children separated from their families by war or other emergency can be reunited with relatives when the crisis recedes. What is required is temporary care in a secure and loving environment, not the permanence of adoption.

I really only want a child without health problems

What was she going to become? How had her parents managed to survive all the hardship and famine?...She was a mystery: her roots, her genetic make-up – everything was hidden from us. It was a case of what we saw was what we got.

Adopter, *From China with Love*

There can be no guarantee about this when you adopt from abroad. There is often very little information available about the child's early experiences and medical history or that of their birth parents, all of which will have implications for the child. Depending on the country of origin, the child may have been exposed to the risk of conditions such as tuberculosis, HIV infection or hepatitis B or C. Reliable and safe testing may not always be available. The child may also have suffered considerable physical, emotional and intellectual deprivation which may have long-term effects. Other factors, for example, the likelihood of any inherited conditions, will probably never be known until they manifest themselves.

What is the process for adopting from overseas?

You must have a home study done by the local authority for the area where you live or by an approved voluntary adoption agency that is also approved as an intercountry adoption agency. It is illegal to commission a private home study report. Many of the issues covered in the home study are the same as those discussed in Chapter 3. The assessment process is similar, including the involvement of the adoption panel. If your adoption agency is in England or Wales, you could also apply, if necessary, to the IRM or IRM Cymru.

Our daughter, Amy, has a serious congenital hearing loss which we didn't know about when we adopted her from China. We love her and we are coping, although we'd always said that we didn't want to adopt a child with a disability.

Adopter

When the adoption agency has approved you as suitable to adopt from your chosen country, the home study report is sent to the Department for Education, the National Assembly for Wales or the Northern Ireland Department of Health, Social Services and Public Safety depending, of course, on where you live.* They will then endorse the application.

* In the rest of this chapter, Department for Education should be read as including the other equivalent bodies around the UK.

Is the process expensive?

Yes, it certainly can be. Most local authorities in the UK, whose first priority must be the placement of children whom they are already looking after, make a charge for the home study to cover their costs. Charges can range from £5,000 to £7,000 or more. There will also be the cost of travel at least once, or possibly more often, to the child's country. Documents need to be translated, there are usually lawyer's fees and charges made by the agency overseas.

In addition, the Department for Education charges applicants in England and Wales a fee for its part of the process. This is means tested and can be up to £1,775 (at the time of writing). Applicants wishing to adopt a close relative from overseas will be exempt.

How do I decide which country to apply to?

The home study must be in relation to one country only and it is for you to decide which one. It is likely to be helpful if this is a country with which you already have links or can make links. It will be important for your child that you have knowledge and understanding of the culture, religion and history of the country and, if possible and realistic, some knowledge of the language. You will need to know, or be prepared to get to know, adults from the country who are willing to play a part in your child's life. It can also be helpful to have contact with other families who have adopted children from that country.

If you cannot accept the culture, customs, food, weather, people or any other aspect of another country then please do not consider adopting from there. That country is going to be part of your life for ever more and you need to support your child in developing a positive self-image based on their birth culture.

Adoptive dad of two children adopted from overseas, *Finding our Familia*

How will I be linked with a child?

The process described here is that for England and Wales. You should enquire locally about the slightly different process in Northern Ireland.

Once the adoption agency has decided on your suitability to adopt and the Department for Education has endorsed the application, the latter will send your papers to an agency in the country you have chosen. The authorities there will decide whether to accept your application and, having done so, your name(s) will be placed on their waiting list for a child. It is the responsibility of the authorities in the child's country of residence to match a child with you.

When the authorities overseas have identified a child for you, they will send you some information about the child, including some medical details. The amount of information provided varies greatly.

When you have received this, it will be important to discuss it with your own GP and you must also discuss it with your social worker. The agency medical adviser may also be able to give you advice. CoramBAAF's leaflet, *Children Adopted from Abroad: Key health and developmental issues*, will also be useful.

When you have made the decision to go ahead with the proposed match, you will need to make arrangements to travel to the child's country to meet the child. If you are then happy to proceed with the adoption, you must notify your adoption agency in writing.

How do I have the child placed with me and bring him or her back to the UK?

The arrangements for this vary according to the adoption laws and procedures of your chosen country, whether the country has ratified or acceded to the Hague Convention and whether or not it is on the UK's list of designated countries. You will need to comply with the requirements of the child's country as well as with UK immigration requirements. Your adoption agency and the other organisations already described can advise you.

Will I have to adopt the child again in the UK?

As described above, this will depend on the country that your child comes from and the arrangements made for the placement in that country. It will be necessary in some situations to apply to adopt to a UK court once you have returned here with the child.

What support will be available after I adopt?

The adoption agency that undertakes your home study should discuss with you what support they can offer after adoption. There are post-adoption centres in England and Wales which can help you and Adoption UK can also provide support (see Useful Organisations). There are also groups of adopters who have adopted children from particular countries. Adoption UK or the Intercountry Adoption Centre should be able to give you information on these.

You may be eligible for financial support through the Adoption Support Fund (ASF). For more information about the ASF, see Chapter 5, "Will support be available after adoption?"

I would like to adopt a child overseas who is related to me

If there has been a crisis in your extended family overseas and, for instance, a child's parents have died suddenly, you can apply for that child to join you in the UK as a dependant. You need to apply to the nearest British diplomatic post in the child's country. If it is agreed that the child has no other family locally able or willing to care for the child, and that the child needs to join you, entry clearance to the UK and indefinite leave to stay may be granted. Once the child has settled with you in the UK, you can decide whether or not adoption would be a good idea.

However, it may be that a relative overseas is planning to help you in your wish to be a parent by giving you one of their children, or you may wish to adopt a child in your extended family overseas who is living in poverty or difficult circumstances. The process in this situation would be to apply to an adoption agency here for a home study, as described earlier in this chapter, but to check out at the same time, through the British diplomatic post in the child's country and the immigration authorities here, whether entry clearance would be likely to be granted. It is unlikely that it would be granted for a child who is being "gifted" to you. Adoption has to be about meeting the needs of a child who is unable to live with their birth parents or other local relatives and who needs to be adopted.

8

What about other options?

Fostering never crossed my mind. I was a chef with no direct experience of parenting or links to the caring professions. Now I'm studying for a certificate in social care, have given up full-time work and am about to become the main carer for five children!

It was my wife Sarah who first suggested fostering. She had worked in a children's residential home. We both liked children and liked the idea of lots of kids passing through the house. We thought we could help them out and pass them on, either to return to their birth family or on to a new, permanent family.

In due course we were approved as temporary foster carers for one or two children aged five to 12. In the end, twins – one girl, one boy – joined the family on the day after their fifth birthday. Caring for children has altered my outlook on life. It's more rewarding than I could ever have dreamt.

Dave, foster carer, CoramBAAF blog

Adoption isn't the only option to provide a loving and secure home for children who cannot live with their birth parents. Alternatives include fostering, special guardianship and a number of legal orders that can secure a child's relationship to their carers.

What is fostering?

Fostering is a way of providing family life for someone else's child in your home. Most of the children looked after by local authorities when their own families are unable to care for them are placed in foster families. There are approximately 64,600 children in foster care in the UK, approximately 70 per cent of all looked after children. Families are unable to care for their children for a variety of reasons. Sometimes parents have physical or mental health issues and have to be hospitalised, or they may misuse drugs or alcohol and need help to overcome their addiction. Children may have been neglected or abused.

Local authorities work with parents to make plans for the children. Parents may have asked for their children to be looked after, or a court may have ordered that a local authority should share responsibility with parents.

I enjoy working with the adults as much as the child. If I had my own children and I was at home with them all day, it would drive me mad. But you go to meetings and get involved with the plans and decisions and you're always working towards things. It's brilliant.

Foster carer, *Growing up in Foster Care*

What about the foster child's parents?

Fostering is shared caring. Foster carers are not the child's legal parents and do not have parental responsibility. They usually share the caring with the child's parents, as well as the local authority. Being a parent whose child is in foster care is painful, and foster carers need to understand this and be sympathetic. Fostered children still have a strong bond with their parents, even if they don't live with them. They often want to see them – or courts may order this – and parents will have a big part to play in making plans for the children's future. It is estimated that 70 per cent of children who are looked after return home within a year.

We've always thought that keeping contact with their birth families whenever possible was a big plus for the children. If all goes well, we will be fine with initiating contact and promoting it. We will work with the family as much as they want and are able to.

Foster carer

Children in foster care can be visited by their parents in a neutral venue, supervised by a social worker. Sometimes part of the task is helping the parent learn to care for the child. Other relatives, like brothers or sisters or grandparents, may also keep in touch with the child.

Could I foster a baby?

You can say which age children you would prefer to foster – if this is babies or small children, you should say so. But it is important to remember that fostering is not a way into adopting a baby or young child. You will be expected to care for the child on a short-term basis until he or she returns home or until other plans are made.

Fostering and adoption

The majority of fostered children return to their families. Many children need help for only a few days or weeks, but others may stay for months or even several years while permanent plans are made and carried out. For some children, adoption becomes the plan and foster carers have an important role in helping the child to move on to their new permanent family.

Fostering does not usually lead to adoption. You have to get used to seeing a child leaving your home, a child you have grown to love. But it can be very satisfying – children who arrive frightened and upset can leave feeling much more confident. Helping a child move on is one of the most important fostering tasks.

We just love having children around. We've got a grown-up daughter and two teenagers at home and we also foster. We like having groups of brothers and sisters and we've got three at the moment. They're aged two, four and five and their social worker has just found adopters for them which is great, although we'll miss them!

Foster carer

Sometimes, however, there might be agreement between the fostering service and yourself that it would be best for a particular child to remain with you or be adopted by you. This would need full and careful discussion and you would need to be re-assessed and approved as an adoptive parent. In 2013/14 in England, 750 children were adopted by their foster carers. If you have fostered a child for a year or more and you want to adopt, it is possible to notify the local authority of your intention to adopt and apply to court for an Adoption Order. However, it is much better to work with the local authority if you can.

In Northern Ireland, adoptive applicants are sometimes approved as foster carers and adopters, and will foster the child pending resolution of the court freeing process.

Fostering for Adoption

See Chapter 4.

Concurrent planning

This is the term given to a small number of schemes currently operating. Children, usually babies or toddlers, for whom there is one last chance that they might return home to their birth family, are placed with families who will foster them with this aim. However, the foster carers are also approved as adopters and will adopt the child, should the planned return home not be successful. In this way, the moves that a child may otherwise have to make are minimised. These schemes operate with the agreement of the local court and to tight timescales.

Families who have children placed under a concurrency scheme have to be prepared to enable very regular contact for the child with their birth family and to be prepared that the child may return home. However, adoption often becomes the plan for these children and the carers can then adopt a child who has been placed with them from a young age. If you might be interested in becoming a carer in a concurrency scheme, First4Adoption can tell you which agencies operate such schemes.

What about long-term fostering?

Sometimes, particularly for children aged 10 or over, foster care may be the plan until the child grows up. This long-term or permanent fostering cannot provide the same legal security as adoption for either the child or the foster family, but it can be the right plan for some children.

Some older children may accept, reluctantly, that they will never be able to return home to live and that they need a new family. However, they may be clear that they do not want to be adopted. They may also need a lot of extra help, for example, special schooling, hospital appointments, or regular therapy sessions. You may decide that you would like to work in partnership with the local authority to offer long-term fostering. The child would remain the legal responsibility of the local authority and of their birth parents.

You would receive a regular fostering allowance as well as being able to call on the local authority for support. Many long-term fostered children are at least nine or 10 years old.

What kind of people become foster carers?

Many different kinds of people are needed to give children a loving and secure foster home. Some foster carers have young children of their own; some are older people whose children are now young adults; others may not have any children of their own. Some are couples and others are single; some are heterosexual and some are gay or lesbian. Some people foster one child at a time, others more than one; some foster only babies or toddlers, others particularly like to look after teenagers. Foster carers come from all walks of life and live in all kinds of homes. It is the job of the social worker to find the right foster carers for each child, and this includes considering cultural and religious factors, among others.

In 28 years, we've never had two children the same. Something that works for one won't work for another. We do a lot of talking with children. We will try things, and see if it works. If one approach isn't working, we need to do something else. You have to change if you want to change the child. We have learnt this over the years.

Foster carer

Would I get paid?

Yes. The fostering allowance covers the cost of feeding, clothing and looking after the child. Fostering allowances vary from area to area and according to the age and needs of the child. Sometimes, foster carers are paid more than just their allowance for looking after a child. They can be paid a fee in recognition of their particular skills and/or because the child whom they are fostering has special needs.

For more information on this subject, see the CoramBAAF book *Thinking about Fostering?* (see Useful Reading), or visit Fostering Network's website at www.thefosteringnetwork.org.uk.

How do I go about fostering a child?

First of all, you need to contact a fostering service covering your area. This could be your local children's services department (England and Wales) or Health and Social Services Trust (Northern Ireland). It could also be a neighbouring one although, as children are usually placed as close as possible to their home area, it is a good idea to apply to an agency as close as possible to where you live. You need to ask to speak to someone in the fostering team.

Independent fostering services also recruit, assess and approve families for fostering.

The Fostering Network has a list of local authority and independent fostering services throughout the UK.

Throughout the assessment we were treated as individuals, it focused on what we'd done before, the strengths we might have to look after children, as well as the difficulties.

Justin and Dan, foster carers, *Recipes for Fostering*

How do I get approved to foster?

Most fostering services run preparation and training groups for prospective foster carers. They will also want to meet with you individually. The whole family will need to be involved. If you have birth children, they will need a chance to think about what fostering will mean for them. Confidential enquiries will be made of your local authority and the police and you will be asked to have a medical examination. The fostering service will prepare a report, with your help, on your application. This report is presented to the service's fostering panel, a group of up to ten people, who include social workers, independent members and at least one foster carer. You should be invited to meet the panel if you wish. The panel makes a recommendation on your application and this goes to a senior manager who makes the final decision. This process usually takes several months.

Getting the training in managing difficult behaviour was a big help. We had this lad who was – I don't know, up and down all the time. Like a pot boiler. After the training I had these new ideas and more confidence, and some of them really worked for him!

Barry, foster carer

What if I'm not approved or if my fostering service wants to end my approval later on?

In this situation, you have a similar right to that of a prospective adopter to apply for an independent review of the proposed decision. You can apply to the Independent Review Mechanism (IRM) England if you live in England, or to the Independent Review Mechanism Cymru if you live in Wales. (See Chapter 3 for more information on the IRM.) The process is much the same as for adopters, except that you have to make the application within 28 days.

What support would I get?

The fostering service must make a foster care agreement with you when you are approved. This covers expectations of both parties and includes the requirement, laid down in regulations, that you should not administer corporal punishment.

As a foster carer, you have to work closely with the child's social worker as well as with the child's birth family. In the early stages this will ensure that you know as much as possible about the child, his or her likes and dislikes, normal routine, favourite foods and toys, etc. Later you will need to discuss the child's progress regularly with the worker and help plan for his or her future.

The local authority must keep records of foster children and foster carers. The local authority and foster carers must make a foster placement agreement, when a child is placed, about matters such as the arrangements for the child's health needs to be met, contact with the birth family and financial support for the child. The local authority must provide foster carers with written information about such things as the child's background, health, and mental and emotional development.

As well as having regular visits from the social workers for the children whom you are fostering, you will have your own supervising social worker, who is there to support and help you in the fostering task. Foster carers are also offered regular ongoing training and there may also be a programme of social events where you and your family can meet other foster families. There are formal Training, Development and Support Standards in England and a similar commitment to the support and training of foster carers in other parts of the UK.

The children whom you foster will have regular reviews, a month after placement, three months after that and then at least every six months. You will be involved in these and your input will be important. All foster carers are also required to have their approval reviewed every year and this provides an opportunity for you to comment on the support you have had.

I see training as part of my support and I accept that I need all the help that I can get to be able to do my job properly and get the most enjoyment out of it.

Foster carer

Special guardianship

Special guardianship is seen as being appropriate when a child or young person and their birth parents do not want to lose the legal link between them but where it is agreed that the child needs permanent new parents who will make all the day-to-day decisions about their care and upbringing. It may be more appropriate than adoption in some situations where children are being permanently cared for by relatives. Special guardianship orders can be revoked by a court and so, while giving a degree of legal security, do not give the complete legal security of adoption. They are valid in England and Wales.

With special guardianship, birth parents do not lose their parental responsibility and so there is still a legal link between the child and them. However, the special guardian acquires parental responsibility which they can exercise to the exclusion of others with parental responsibility in all but a very few instances (for example, agreement to a change of name or to adoption).

Special guardians whose child was looked after by the local authority before the order was made are entitled to ask to be assessed for a range of support services, including financial support. These support services are similar to those available to adoptive parents and include eligibility to apply to the Adoption Support Fund (ASF) for financial support for therapeutic services. For more information about the ASF see Chapter 5, "Will support be available after adoption?"

If you are a foster carer and think that special guardianship might be appropriate, you should talk to the child's social worker and/or to a solicitor with experience of child care law.

The process for applying for special guardianship is to notify the local authority in writing of your intention. Three months later you can apply to a Magistrates' Family Proceedings Court, the County Court or the High Court, provided the child has lived with you for at least one year. The local authority is required to prepare a report for the court. You should ensure as far as possible that your support needs are fully discussed and agreed at this stage, although you can apply for these to be further assessed after the order has been made, if necessary.

The CoramBAAF leaflet, *Special Guardianship: Some questions answered* provides more information (see Useful Reading).

I did not want to adopt my own grandchild...Remember, this is family...So guardianship seemed to be a nicer way of going forward and provided a bit more control for us.

Grandparent, *Special Guardianship in Practice*

Child Arrangements Orders in England and Wales

Child Arrangements Orders (CAO) are only a legal option in England and Wales. They give people looking after a child more day-to-day rights than foster carers have, but not as many as adopters or special guardians. The birth parents are still legally involved and retain parental responsibility, but the holders of the Order acquire it too. Foster carers can apply for a CAO even if the child's parents or local authority are not in agreement, provided that the child has lived with them for at least 12 months. The local authority can pay a CAO allowance, but is not obliged to do so. A CAO usually lasts until the child is 18. If you want to know more about this Order, you should talk to your local authority or a solicitor with experience of child care law.

Residence Orders in Northern Ireland

Residence Orders (RO) are only a legal option in Northern Ireland. They give people looking after a child more day-to-day rights than foster carers have, but not as many as adopters or special guardians. The birth parents are still legally involved and retain parental responsibility, but the holders of the Order acquire it too. Foster carers can apply for a RO even if the child's parents or local authority are not in agreement, provided that the child has lived with them for three years. The Trust can pay an RO allowance, but is not obliged to do so. An RO usually lasts until the child is 16. If you want to more about this Order, you should talk to your local Trust or a solicitor with experience of child care law.

Private fostering

Some parents make private arrangements for their children to be looked after by private foster carers who are not approved and registered with the local authority in the same way as the foster carers described in the rest of this chapter. There are special regulations for private fostering (see the CoramBAAF leaflet, *Private Fostering: Some questions answered*, listed in Useful Reading).

9

Stepchildren and adoption

When my husband and I divorced, Jordan was only one-and-a-half and continued to live with me. A few years later I remarried and David and I had Julia. We really wanted the four of us to be a family. David wanted to adopt Jordan but, after talking this through with Jordan, who still saw her father regularly, we realised that this would not be right for her. We are now thinking of applying for a Child Arrangements Order.

Mother

ENGLAND AND WALES

You are a stepfamily if you or your partner have a child from a previous relationship who is living with you. It is estimated that around 10 per cent of dependent children in England and Wales live in a stepfamily at any one time. Only a very small proportion of these children are adopted each year, about 435 children.

Most stepfamilies don't adopt. The adults involved work out satisfactory arrangements for the care and upbringing of the children, who will often have contact with the family members with whom they are not living. However, if you are considering adoption, the following information may be helpful. You may also want to read CoramBAAF's leaflet *Stepchildren and Adoption* (see Useful Reading).

Are there other ways to help make the child secure in our family?

A parental responsibility agreement or Order

The Adoption and Children Act 2002, which came into force in 2005, introduced this option for step-parents. It is available to a step-parent who is married to, or has entered into a civil registration with, the child's birth parent. A step-parent may acquire parental responsibility for the child by a simple but formal agreement with the parent who is his or her partner and with the other parent if he or she has parental responsibility. The agreement must be recorded on an official form and signed by each parent with parental responsibility and the step-parent, in front of a court official. Copies must be lodged at the Principal Registry of the Family Division. The official form and guidance notes can be obtained from the Court Service at www.hmcourts-service.gov.uk.

If the non-resident parent who has parental responsibility will not enter into this agreement, an application can be made for a Parental Responsibility Order to a Magistrates' Family Proceedings Court, the County Court or the High Court. There is no need to give prior notice to the local authority but the court may ask for a report about the child's welfare.

A parental responsibility agreement or order does not take parental responsibility away from parents who already have it.

A Child Arrangements Order (England and Wales) (see Chapter 8)

This is a court order in England and Wales which can set out with whom the child is to reside (or live). It also gives the step-parent who acquires it parental responsibility for the child. However, it doesn't take parental responsibility away from anyone else who has it, for example, the child's mother or the non-resident father if the parents were married when the child was born or if he has acquired parental responsibility. In effect, the child would have three parents with responsibility for ensuring his or her welfare. A step-parent does not need to be married to, or in a civil partnership with, the child's parent before applying for a Child Arrangements Order. You can apply for a Child Arrangements Order to your local Magistrates' Family Proceedings Court, the County Court or the High Court. It wouldn't prevent you applying for an Adoption Order at a later stage if you wish.

It is also important for the parent with whom the child is living to make a will, appointing a guardian for the child in the event of his or her death. If the step-parent is appointed and has a Child Arrangements Order, the child will stay with him or her should their birth parent die.

A similar Order called a Residence Order applies in Northern Ireland (See Chapter 8).

We'd like the child to have the same surname as us

You don't have to adopt the child to achieve this. If the child's parents were married or the father has acquired parental responsibility, the child's surname cannot be changed without the agreement of the non-resident parent, unless a court gives permission. However, if the child's parents were not married and the father does not have parental responsibility, the child's surname can be changed with the agreement of his or her mother either by common usage, or by a statutory declaration or by deed poll. You should consult a citizen's advice bureau or solicitor about this. Obviously your child's wishes should be taken into account. Many children now live in families where there are a number of different surnames and they may be quite happy with this and want to retain their own birth surname.

Does the child's other parent have to be contacted and agree to an Order?

If the other parent is the mother, or is a father who was married to the child's mother or who has acquired parental responsibility, his or her agreement to an Order is necessary. A court considering an application can dispense with the parent's agreement but would need compelling reasons to do so. If the child's birth father was not married to the mother and does not have parental responsibility, his formal agreement is not necessary. However, the court would want to know what his views were and would usually require efforts to have been made to seek these. The court would consider the father's views in relation to the part he has played, or wished to play, in the child's life.

Does the child have to know what is happening?

Yes. The court will want to know what the child's views are. This would apply to children of three or so, and older. The court would want assurances that younger children will be told the truth about their parentage and about the adoption. This should usually start from when the child is about three, so that they grow up always having known.

Do we have to be married before the step-parent can adopt?

No, the step-parent does not have to be married to their partner. However, they must have been living with them and the child for at least six months. The step-parent can apply for an Adoption Order and, if granted, this will give him or her the same parental rights as their partner, the resident birth parent, while taking away the parental responsibility and rights of any parent or other person who previously had this.

What is the process for applying to adopt?

You must notify the local authority where you live of your intention to adopt. It can be useful to arrange to speak to a social worker in children's services to discuss whether adoption will be a good plan. If you decide to go ahead, you must wait three months after notifying the local authority of your intention and then you need to apply to a local Magistrates' Family Proceedings Court, to a County Court or to the High Court. There will be a fee to pay and you will need to complete an application form. The court will require a social worker in the local authority to produce a full report for the court hearing. This will involve interviews with you both, with your children and with the other parent and this process should start once you notify the local authority of your intention to apply to adopt. On the basis of this report, the court will decide whether or not to make an Adoption Order. This process need not take longer than about three months, but can often take up to a year, depending on the circumstances of the case and the workload of the children's services department and the court.

NORTHERN IRELAND

With the consent of a non-resident birth parent with parental rights and responsibilities, a step-parent may adopt, but must do this jointly with the child's resident birth parent, to whom he or she must be married.

At first I got on really well with my stepfather and wanted him to adopt me...But when I was a teenager it was nothing but rows over everything I did. Then I wished he hadn't adopted me! But we're OK now.

Adopted young person, *Stepchildren and Adoption*

10

Finding an adoption agency

The decision to adopt, or even to make that first phone call, isn't at all straightforward. It's the beginning of an unknown journey. I've always been a slightly nervous traveller. I like to know exactly what the arrangements are and to get to the airport in plenty of time. But the adoption journey is more of a mystery tour. There was no child in mind when we embarked on the process. It's a bit like deciding to get married without having a specific partner in mind…

I phoned up on the Monday and had an informal chat with one of the social workers. He arranged to send out some information and a form to fill in if we wanted to ask for an initial visit. The form duly came and we completed it and returned it the next weekend. By that stage, our interest had solidified and we'd psyched ourselves up to go forward seriously.

Robert, adoptive dad, *The Family Business*

Do I have to go through an adoption agency?

Unless you are a close relative of the child you want to adopt, you must apply to an adoption agency. There are over 200 adoption agencies in the UK. Most of these are based in local authority children's services departments in England and Wales. In Northern Ireland, these services are provided by Health and Social Care Trusts.

There are also voluntary adoption agencies, which can vary widely in size. Some are large national organisations, such as Barnardo's. Others are regional. Some of these are linked to churches, for example, the Catholic Children's Society. Some agencies focus on recruiting families for certain groups of waiting children, such as older children, disabled children, or sibling groups, so it is important to find out before you apply. Local authority adoption agencies covering large areas tend to take applications mainly from people within their area. However, agencies which are geographically small, for example, London boroughs, often prefer not to recruit adopters from their own area as they will tend to live too close to the birth families of the children who need placement.

Voluntary adoption agencies usually cover a wider area than the local authorities do, often including several counties. So it is worth contacting voluntary adoption agencies in counties near to your own, as well as any in it.

You are not limited to your own immediate locality, but most agencies work roughly within a 50-mile radius of their office. There can be a lot of travelling involved in the process, from your initial meeting with an agency, right through to assessment and introductions with a child so working with an agency which is close to you will be useful. It is important to remember that you and your child will need help and support from the agency after placement. It is much harder for an agency to give you adequate support if they are based a long way away and you should discuss what their plans are for this before you decide to work with them.

*Picking up the phone the first time to admit to someone in
authority that we wanted to adopt was surprisingly hard. I felt
nervous – it was like nothing else I'd ever done before.*

Adopter, *The Pink Guide to Adoption*

Would it be best to apply to the local authority or to a voluntary adoption agency?

Voluntary agencies tend to be small and to specialise in adoption and
fostering work. They are often able to give very good support once a
child is placed with you. Local authorities are bigger and have to
respond to a wide range of needs. However, they are the agencies
responsible for placing children and will usually consider families
whom they have approved first. They may expect you to wait for up
to three months after you are approved for the placement of a child
looked after by them before referring you to an Adoption Register or
consortium and before you respond to children from other local
authorities whom you may see needing a new family. Voluntary
agencies will actively help you to try and find a child, through using
an Adoption Register or consortium, family-finding services and
other contacts. So, there can be advantages and disadvantages in
working with either type of agency.

How to find an adoption agency

Adoption UK publishes a useful directory of adoption agencies
that is searchable by postcode. It is available on their website:
www.adoptionuk.org/about-adoption/find-agency-near-you.

If you live in England, you could also contact First4Adoption, a
national information service on adoption in England (see Useful
Organisations). They also have a searchable directory of all adoption

agencies in England on their website: www.first4adoption.org.uk. The National Adoption Service Wales has a similar list for Wales: www.adoptcymru.com

You can also search online for adoption agencies in your area, including your local authority.

When you have found one or more agencies that are reasonably near you, the next step is to phone or email them for further information. Official guidance states that you should expect to receive written information in response to your enquiry within five working days.

Adoption agencies run regular information events, usually involving social workers and adoptive parents. They are a good way of finding out more about how the agency works and, if this is a local authority agency, the kind of children whom they are looking to place.

It is worth contacting several agencies before making a decision as it is important that you feel comfortable with whichever agency you decide to go ahead with. You will be working with them for a long time, throughout your assessment, and later on when you are matched. You need to feel comfortable with your social worker as it will make it easier when you look at aspects of your life in detail together during the assessment process.

Agencies will have their own priorities – including finding the right families for children in their care if it is a local authority agency. If an agency isn't willing to take your application forward, don't feel discouraged. Speak to other agencies until you find one who is interested in discussing your application.

You can contact a number of agencies at this early stage. However, you can make a firm application and enter into the preparation and assessment process with only one agency.

Conclusion

We hope that this book has helped to answer any questions you may have about adoption. There are many organisations available if you need more information, some of which are listed in Useful Organisations. If you decide to choose adoption as the route to creating a family, there is a great deal of help available, and you won't be expected to go it alone. Many specialist organisations and self-help groups can offer support and advice to help you in your adoption journey.

The most important things in adoption are the families it creates and the children it helps, and so the last words go to them.

Being a parent, whether by birth or adoption, is not an easy job...but at the end of a hard day, it all becomes worthwhile when a voice says, 'You are the best mum in the whole world.'

Pamela, adoptive mum

My feelings about adoption

Adoption is the best thing ever, to me. It gives children a second chance. How it's happened to me, I feel like the luckiest boy alive. I am so happy someone picked me to be part of their family. On the day I was to meet my forever mum and dad I was very excited, but scared as well, because I didn't know if we would like each other. I hid behind my older brother. Now I have been with my forever mum and dad for five years. I still don't regret going to live with them. Today I never look back and my forever parents feel like my real parents, and I love them more than anything in the world.

Sid, age 11

Useful organisations

First4Adoption

A dedicated service for people interested in adopting a child in England. First4Adoption's website provides advice about adoption, agency contact details and other information such as listings for agency information evenings around England. Those interested in adoption can sign up for an email newsletter.

Information line: 10am–6pm Monday–Friday
Tel: 0300 222 0022
www.first4adoption.org.uk

National Adoption Service Wales

The National Adoption Service was created to improve services for all those affected by adoption in Wales. Its website has information about how to adopt and contact details for adoption services in Wales.

Room 409 County Hall
Atlantic Wharf
Cardiff CF10 4UW
Tel: 029 2087 3927
www.adoptcymru.com

Adoption UK

A parent-to-parent network of over 3,500 established and potential adoptive families. It welcomes enquiries from prospective adopters; offers local support groups across the UK; publishes a range of useful leaflets and a monthly magazine written by and for adopters, which also features children waiting for adoption.

Units 11 and 12
Vantage Business Park
Bloxham Road
Banbury OX16 9UX
Tel: 01295 752240
www.adoptionuk.org.uk.

FAMILY-FINDING ORGANISATIONS

Adoption Register for England

A database of waiting approved adopters and children for whom adoption is the plan. Only adoption agencies in England refer adopters and children to the Register.

The Register has two main elements. Firstly, there is the computer database that stores the details of children waiting and families approved. Secondly, there is a team of experienced database operators and social workers who use the information to suggest potential matches between children and prospective adopters. Local authority adoption agencies are expected to refer children for whom adoption is the plan three months after this decision has been made, if a local match has not been identified. They must also refer prospective adopters three months after their approval, if they have not already had a child matched. Although they are not obliged to do so, most voluntary adoption agencies also refer adopters they have approved. All families must give consent before they can be referred and can also refer themselves three months after approval.

Prospective adopters can contact Register staff directly for general advice, and to check that they are on referral and their details are correct. They will be informed if their details have been sent out as a possible link, but will be advised to contact their social worker for further details about the child involved.

The Register also holds family-finding activities such as Adoption Exchange Days.

At the time of writing, a pilot project is under way to allow prospective adopters to search children's details directly.

Unit 4, Pavilion Business Park
Royds Hall Road, Wortley
Leeds LS12 6AJ
Adopters' helpline: 0345 222 9058
www.adoptionregister.org.uk

Wales Adoption Register

A database of waiting approved adopters and children for whom adoption is the plan. Only adoption agencies in Wales refer adopters and children to the Register.

Similarly to the Adoption Register in England, it holds a database of all children in Wales who are waiting to be adopted and of all approved adopters in Wales who have not yet been matched with a child. Details of children that need families and of approved adopters are kept on the Adoption Register database. The team uses the database information to identify potential matches between children and prospective adopters.

The Register also holds family-finding activities such as Adoption Exchange Days.

c/o City of Cardiff Council
Room 329 County Hall
Atlantic Wharf
Cardiff CF10 4UW
Adopter helpline: 029 2087 3799
www.walesadoptionregister.org.uk

Adoption Regional Information System for Northern Ireland (ARIS)

A national linking service for children and families in Northern Ireland. It operates in a similar way to the Adoption Register for England and Wales.

Directorate of Social Care and Children
Health and Social Care Board
Level 3
12–22 Linenhall Street
Belfast BT2 8BS
Tel: 028 9536 3098
http://online.hscni.net/aris/

Children who Wait

An online matching service, also published as a monthly magazine, run by Adoption UK. The website and magazine feature profiles of children who need adoption, in any area of the UK. The magazine is automatically sent out to subscribing members each month. It is complemented by the online service that contains additional information about the children, extra photos and film clips. To subscribe, you have to become a member of Adoption UK (see details earlier in this section).

Tel: 01295 752240
www.adoptionuk.org.uk

Link Maker

An online family-finding service run by adoptive parents, which helps agencies find adoption and fostering matches for children. Adopters and foster carers can register for family-finding and to access support. The service also has chatrooms and support groups for adopters, and information about adoption and fostering.

Tel: 0843 886 0040
www.linkmaker.co.uk

OTHER ORGANISATIONS

CoramBAAF

An organisation for all those working in the adoption, fostering and childcare fields. CoramBAAF gives advice and information on adoption, fostering and childcare issues; publishes a wide range of books, training resources and leaflets as well as a quarterly journal on adoption, fostering and childcare issues; provides training and consultancy services to social workers and other professionals to help them improve the quality of services to children and families; gives evidence to government committees on subjects concerning children and families; and responds to consultation documents on changes in legislation and regulations.

Most local authorities and voluntary adoption agencies are members of CoramBAAF. You can join CoramBAAF as an individual member; visit the website for details.

41 Brunswick Square
London WC1N 1AZ
Tel: 020 7520 0300
www.corambaaf.org.uk

Contact a Family

A charity for any parent or professional involved with or caring for a child with disabilities. Through a network of mutual support and self-help groups, Contact a Family brings together families whose children have disabilities, and offers advice to parents who wish to start a support group.

209–211 City Road
London EC1V 1JN
Helpline: 0808 808 3555
www.cafamily.org.uk

Infertility Network UK

The national self-help organisation which provides information, support and representation to people with fertility difficulties and those who work with them.

Charter House
43 St Leonards Road
Bexhill on Sea
East Sussex TN40 1JA
Helpline: 01424 732361
www.infertilitynetworkuk.com

Intercountry Adoption Centre

Offers advice and information about current policy and practice in relation to overseas adoption and the legal requirements of the UK and "sending" countries. It produces a useful information pack with information about particular countries, and also runs group events.

22 Union Street
Barnet
Hertfordshire
EN5 4HZ
Tel: 020 8447 4753
www.icacentre.org.uk

Independent Review Mechanism England and Independent Review Mechanism Cymru

Independent Review Mechanism (IRM) England
Unit 4 Pavilion Business Park
Royds Hall Road
Wortley
Leeds
LS12 6AJ
Tel: 0845 450 3956
www.independentreviewmechanism.org.uk

Independent Review Mechanism Cymru
Head Office
25 Windsor Place
Cardiff CF10 3BZ
Tel:029 2034 2434
http://irm.cymru/

Useful reading

These publications are available from CoramBAAF. Visit www.corambaaf.org.uk or contact CoramBAAF Publications on 020 7520 7517 for more details or to order.

BOOKS ABOUT ADOPTION

PERSONAL NARRATIVES BY ADOPTERS

Our Adoption Journey
JAYNE LILLEY

An enthralling real-life account that follows Jayne, Dan and their son Charlie through the assessment and preparation process and their adoption of a Jessie, their young adopted daughter. Includes details of the new two-stage assessment process in England and Wales.

An Adoption Diary
MARIA JAMES

This is an inspirational real-life account of one couple's emotional journey to become a family, which gives a fascinating insight into adoption today. Spanning four years, the diary covers assessment, the months of waiting, and finally the match with a two-year-old boy.

Flying Solo
JULIA WISE

Julia Wise gave up a high-flying career and hectic London life to move to the country and adopt a child on her own. This heart-warming and humorous account will resonate loudly with single adopters everywhere.

In Black and White
NATHALIE SEYMOUR

This honest account follows Nathalie and Tom, a white couple living in 1970s Britain, who decided to establish a transracial adopted family. Further, they wanted the children to remain connected with their birth family. An intriguing and absorbing story.

Adoption Undone
KAREN CARR

This is the true story of an adoption and an adoption breakdown, bravely told by the adoptive mother. From the final court hearing when Lucy returned to local authority care, Karen Carr looks back over a tale of loss and regret, but also courage, generosity and self-discovery.

Together in Time
RUTH AND ED ROYCE

From a dual perspective, each with their own anxieties and expectations, Ruth and Ed Royce record their decision to adopt, their son's deep-seated problems, and how their experience of music and art therapy helped them to come together as a family…and to adopt for a second time.

The Family Business
ROBERT MARSDEN

This is the story of the adoption of William, a little boy with cerebral palsy, by a middle-aged couple with three birth children. Narrated by the adoptive father, this positive, upbeat account describes adopting a child with a disability and the impact of adoption on the whole family.

Take Two
LAUREL ASHTON

This moving story follows Laurel and David through their discovery of their infertility, months of treatment, and eventual decision to adopt. Their adoption of Amber, a baby girl, and then of Emily, are narrated, as Laurel remembers the first months of family life.

Dale's Tale
HELEN JAYNE

The story of Helen, a foster carer, and her family, and what happened when a short-term foster placement – of Dale, a young boy – became longer than expected. When Helen decides she wants to adopt Dale, the agencies involved have other ideas.

Holding on and Hanging in
JACKIE WHITE

This compelling journey tracks Wayne's journey, from first being fostered by Lorna at the age of nine, in a "therapeutic" foster placement, through nearly four years of family life. Wayne is traumatised by his early experiences, and helping him to heal and grow is a long and difficult process, but Lorna is determined to persevere.

Frozen
MIKE BUTCHER

When husband and wife Mike and Lesley embark on a course of IVF treatment, they are full of hope for a successful outcome – a child they can call their own. But after a shocking reaction to the treatment, and an escalating series of setbacks and heartache, they are forced to put their dream on hold – until they look into adoption.

When Daisy met Tommy
JULES BELLE

This is the real-life story of how six-year-old Daisy and her parents adopted Tom. Honest and accessible, it charts the ups and downs of the adoption process, as experienced by a daughter already in the family.

Becoming Dads
PABLO FERNÁNDEZ

This is the story of Pablo and Mike, and their journey to adoption. Set against a backdrop of diverse perceptions as to whether gay men should adopt, Pablo's narrative tracks them through approaching an agency, being approved, and finally adopting a young boy.

Is it True you have Two Mums?
RUBY CLAY
The heartwarming story of Ruby and Gail, who adopt three
daughters, through different routes, as a lesbian dual-heritage
couple.

Finding our Familia
STEVAN WHITEHEAD
Stevan Whitehead tells the story of his family's adoption of two
children from Guatemala, but also their many subsequent trips to the
country, their supportive links with their new-found extended family,
and the way they help their children maintain links with their origins.

PARENTING MATTERS SERIES

This series of books looks at a number of health needs and
conditions that are often associated with looked after children.
Authoritative information about the condition and how it affects
children is followed by personal stories from adopters or carers that
describe day-to-day life with an affected child. The series covers a
range of conditions, including:

- *Parenting a Child with Attention Deficit Hyperactivity Disorder*
- *Parenting a Child with Dyslexia*
- *Parenting a Child with Mental Health Issues*
- *Parenting a Child Affected by Parenting Substance Misuse*
- *Parenting a Child with Emotional and Behavioural Difficulties*
- *Parenting a Child with Autism Spectrum Disorder*
- *Parenting a Child with Developmental Delay*
- *Parenting a Child with or at risk of a Genetic Disease*
- *Parenting a Child Affected by Domestic Violence*
- *Parenting a Child Affected by Sexual Abuse*
- *Parenting a Child who has Experienced Trauma*

ADOPTION: DIFFERENT ASPECTS

The Adopter's Handbook
AMY NEIL SALTER
This guide sets out clear, accurate information about adoption before, during and after the big event, to help adopters help themselves throughout the adoption process and beyond. Topics covered include education, health and adoption support.

Attachment, Trauma and Resilience
KATE AND BRIAN CAIRNS
Drawing on Kate's and Brian's personal experiences with three birth children and 12 fostered children, this book describes family life with children who have experienced attachment difficulties, loss and trauma. Using knowledge and ideas drawn from attachment theory, the authors suggest practical ideas about what can be done to promote recovery and develop resilience.

Related by Adoption: A handbook for grandparents and other carers
HEDI ARGENT
This handbook aims to give grandparents and other relatives information about adoption today that directly affects them. It discusses how the wider family can support building a family through adoption and be involved in both the good and the bad times.

Chosen: Writing and poetry by adopted children and young people
EDITED BY PERLITA HARRIS
Intensely moving, this collection of prose, poetry and artwork from 80 adopted children and young people, aged from 4 to 20 years of age, reveals how it feels and what it means to be adopted.

ADOPTION: PARENTING

Why was I Adopted?
JANE JACKSON
A short guide that looks at some of the most common big adoption
questions that adopted children ask, and explores the feelings and
worries that can lie behind the questions, with suggested dialogues.

Talking about Adoption to your Adopted Child
MARJORIE MORRISON
A guide to the whys, whens, and hows of telling adopted children
about their origins at different ages and stages and including a range
of subjects.

Adoption Conversations: What, when and how to tell
RENÉE WOLFS
This in-depth practical guide, written by an adoptive parent, explores
the questions adopted children are likely to ask, with suggestions for
helpful answers. Although the guide focuses primarily on children
adopted from abroad, the advice is applicable to any adopted child.
A second book, *More Adoption Conversations*, by the same author,
looks at adopted young people aged 13–18.

Looking After our Own: The stories of black and Asian
adopters
EDITED BY HOPE MASSIAH
An inspiring collection looking at the experiences of nine black and
Asian adoptive families and their children.

FORM ICA

Intercountry adoption form (medical report and development
assessment of child) which, when ordered individually, comes with
two copies of Form AH for the prospective adoptive parents.

ADVICE NOTES

CoramBAAF's popular leaflet series contains essential information about key areas in adoption and fostering.

Adoption – some questions answered
Basic information about adoption. Explains the adoption process including the legal issues and the rights of birth parents.

Foster care – some questions answered
Basic information about fostering. Explains different types of foster care and the relationship with the local authority.

The preparation and assessment process (adoption)
Aimed at prospective adopters who have started the process with an agency. Explores preparation and assessment and what it involves. Available free online to CoramBAAF members.

The preparation and assessment process (fostering)
Aimed at prospective foster carers who have started the process with an agency. Explores preparation and assessment and what it involves. Available free online to CoramBAAF members.

Children's special needs – some questions answered
Information on the special needs that adopted and fostered children may have, for people considering adopting or fostering.

Private fostering
Aimed at those considering private fostering in England and Wales, this leaflet explains what private fostering involves, and what prospective carers need to know.

Special guardianship
Provides information about the difference between special guardianship and other forms of permanence for children.

Stepchildren and adoption
Information for birth parents and step-parents on the advantages or not of adoption, and obtaining further advice. Editions available for England and Wales or Scotland.

Intercountry adoption – information and guidance
Information on adopting a child from overseas, including procedures, legislation, and where to obtain advice.

Children adopted from abroad – key health and developmental issues
Gives advice on the health and medical issues you may encounter if adopting a child from overseas. Available free online to CoramBAAF members.

CoramBAAF produces a wide variety of other books about adoption, including a large selection of books for use with children. For more details, visit www.corambaaf.org.uk or contact 020 7520 7517.

Glossary

Below is a glossary of certain terms that appear in this book. Where there is a difference between UK countries, this is shown.

Accommodation/accommodated

The local authority must 'provide accommodation' for children in need in certain circumstances. The local authority does not acquire parental responsibility merely by accommodating a child and the arrangements must normally be agreed with the parent(s), who, subject to certain circumstances, are entitled to remove the child at any time. They keep parental responsibility. A child who is accommodated is a looked after child.

Adoption panel

Adoption agencies must set up an adoption panel to consider and make recommendations on children for whom adoption is the plan, on prospective adopters and on matches between prospective adopters and children.

Adoption and permanence panel

Many local authorities have panels which, in addition to considering adoption, also consider and make recommendations about long-term fostering. Some in England and Wales also consider special guardianship cases.

Adoption Placement Plan

A term used in England. A plan that gives information to the prospective adopter about the child when the agency has decided to place the child with them. It sets out, for example, when the child will move into the prospective adopter's home, parental responsibility, adoption support services, contact with the child, and arrangements for reviewing the placement.

Adoption Placement Report

A term used in England. A report prepared by the adoption agency for the adoption panel which sets out, for example, the reasons for proposing the placement, arrangement for allowing any person contact with the child, the prospective adopter's view on the proposed placement, and, where the agency is a local authority, proposals for providing adoption support services for the adoptive family.

Adoption Register

Database of approved prospective adopters and children waiting for adoption. There are separate Registers in England, Wales and Scotland, and a similar arrangement in Northern Ireland (ARIS). A team of experienced social workers use the database to suggest links for children with approved prospective adopters where local matches cannot be found. In England, the Register is run by Adoption Match on behalf of the Government, and at the time of writing (2016), a pilot project is under way to allow prospective adopters to search children's details directly.

Adoption Regional Information System (ARIS)

A scheme similar to the Adoption Register, for approved adopters and children living in Northern Ireland.

Adoption support agency (ASA) – England and Wales

An organisation or person registered to provide adoption support services. An ASA may operate on a profit or not-for-profit basis.

Adult Attachment Interview (AAI)

A tool for assessing an adult's attachment style, based on asking about the adult's experience of being parented. It is used by trained assessors, largely as a research tool.

Annex A Report

A court report in relation to an adoption application in England.

Article 15 Report

A report prepared on a prospective adopter under Article 15 of the Hague Convention. This includes information on their identity, eligibility and suitability to adopt, background, family and medical history, social environment, reasons for adoption, ability to undertake an intercountry adoption and the characteristics of the children for whom they would be qualified to care.

Article 16 Information

A report prepared on the child under Article 16 of the Hague Convention. This includes information on his/her identity, adoptability, background, social environment, family history, medical history including that of the child's family, and any special needs of the child.

Attachment Style Interview (ASI)

A standardised assessment tool, developed at Royal Holloway, University of London, which can be used to assess the characteristics of carers in terms of their quality of close relationships, social support and security of attachment style. It assesses particularly the adequacy of support and the carer's ability to access support. It should only be used by trained assessors.

CAFCASS – England

The Children and Family Court Advisory and Support Service is a national non-departmental public body for England. CAFCASS is independent of the courts, social services, education and health authorities and all similar agencies. A CAFCASS officer must normally witness the consent to adoption of a birth parent. When courts are dealing with cases involving children's welfare, they often appoint a CAFCASS children's guardian to make enquiries and report to the court on behalf of the child.

CAMHS (Child and Adolescent Mental Health Services)

Services that contribute to the mental health care of children and young people, whether provided by health, education or social services or other agencies. CAMHS covers all types of provision and intervention including individual therapy for children, mental health promotion and primary prevention and specialist community-based services.

Care order – England and Wales

A child who is subject to a care order is described as being "in care". A care order is a court order that gives the local authority parental responsibility for the child but does not deprive the parent(s) of this. Nevertheless, the local authority may limit the extent to which parents may exercise their parental responsibility and may override parental wishes in the interests of the child.

Care Plan – England and Wales

All children who are the subject of care proceedings must have a written care plan, which is presented to the court. If the plan for the child is adoption, this plan must include the details of any proposed placement or the programme for how such a placement is to be found. This could include referral to the Adoption Register.

Child Arrangements Order – England and Wales

A court order that was introduced in the Children and Families Act 2014 and came into force in April 2014. It replaced Residence Orders and Contact Orders. The Order will set out the arrangements for the person(s) with whom the child is to live. Where a Child Arrangements Order (CAO) is made in favour of someone who does not already have parental responsibility for the child (e.g. a relative or foster carer), that person will acquire parental responsibility subject to certain restrictions (e.g. they will not be able to consent to the child's adoption). Parental responsibility given in connection with a CAO will only last as long as the Order is in force. A CAO can last until the child's 18th birthday. A CAO discharges a Care Order. However, a birth parent with parental responsibility retains this and shares it with the holder of the CAO.

Child Arrangements Order allowance – England and Wales

Local authorities have a power to contribute to the cost of a child's maintenance when the child is living with somebody under a CAO, provided he or she is not living with a parent or step-parent. A financial contribution under this power is normally referred to as a CAO allowance.

Child's Permanence Report (CPR)

A report required under English regulations when adoption is the plan for a child. It should include comprehensive information on the child, their birth family, the reasons for the adoption plan, proposed contact arrangements, and the views of the birth parents and child on the plan.

Children's Guardian

A person working for CAFCASS who is appointed by the court to safeguard a child's interests in court proceedings. Their duties include presenting a report to the court. The guardian is an experienced qualified social worker who is independent of the local authority. He or she will support the child, birth parents, social workers and others, read reports, etc, before reaching a view on the case.

Concurrent planning

The term given to a small number of schemes currently operating. Children, usually babies or toddlers, for whom there is a chance that they might return home to their birth family, are placed with families who will foster them with this aim. However, the foster carers are also approved as adopters and will adopt the child, should the planned return home not be successful. In this way, the moves that a child may otherwise have to make are minimised. These schemes have to be run with the agreement and co-operation of the local court and to tight timescales.

Consortium

A group of local adoption agencies, often both local authorities and voluntary adoption agencies, which share details of waiting families and children in order to try to make speedy local placements for children.

Contact

Contact may be used to mean visits, including residential visits or other form of direct face-to-face contact, between a child and another individual, or it may mean indirect ways of keeping in touch (e.g. letters or telephone calls including letters sent via a third party).

Couple

Two people (whether of different sexes or the same sex) living as partners (married or unmarried) in an enduring family relationship. This does not include two people, one of whom is the other's parent, grandparent, sister, brother, aunt or uncle.

Decision maker

A senior person within the fostering service or adoption agency or a trustee or director of the fostering service or voluntary adoption agency with experience in child care social work. In England and Wales they are specifically required to have at least three years' post-qualifying experience in this area of work. The decision maker receives reports, agreed panel minutes and recommendations and makes the final decision on cases presented to the panel.

Disclosure and Barring Service (DBS)

An agency that provides access to criminal records and other information. In relation to adoption and fostering, the DBS provides enhanced disclosures on prospective adopters and foster carers and members of their households to the adoption or fostering agency.

Disruption

A term used to describe adoptions or permanent foster placements that do not work out. When a placement disrupts the child is returned to the care of the agency that originally placed him or her or, if he or she is adopted, is looked after by the local authority where the adoptive family lives. A disruption meeting should be convened, followed by counselling or other support for the family. If the child has been legally adopted, the adoptive parents retain parental responsibility until the child is re-adopted by new parents, should this be the plan.

Fast-track approval process

This is available to any approved foster carer in England and to people who have previously adopted in a court in England or Wales under the Adoption Agencies Regulations 2005 (or Welsh equivalent). It enables these individuals to enter the adoption approval process at Stage Two. Agencies must complete the process within four months.

Foster care/fostering

Cases where a child is placed with a foster carer by the local authority or (in rare cases) placed directly by a voluntary organisation. "Short-term", "long-term" and "permanent" foster care and "respite care" (also known as "short breaks") may mean different things to different people; they are not legally defined terms.

Fostering for Adoption (FfA)

Under Fostering for Adoption, an agency can give an approved adopter temporary approval as a foster carer for a named child. This enables a child to be placed as a foster child with carers without them having had a full fostering assessment or panel approval. These will be children for whom the likelihood of eventual adoption is high. However, the child is fostered until, in most cases, work with birth parents and court involvement enables an adoption plan to be agreed and the child to be matched for adoption with these carers at panel.

Independent Review Mechanism (IRM) England

The IRM England is a review process conducted by a independent panel that prospective adopters and foster carers can use when they have been given a qualifying determination by an agency that they are not going to be approved as an adoptive parent/foster carer. This includes cases where the agency decides to withdraw an approval previously given. The review panel reviews the case and gives a recommendation to the agency. The agency decision-maker then makes the final decision.

Independent Review Mechanism (IRM) Cymru

This is only available to people assessed by an agency in Wales. It operates in the same way as the IRM for England, described above.

Independent Reviewing Officer (IRO) – England and Wales

The IRO must chair statutory child care reviews and ensure that reviews are timely. They must monitor the effectiveness, appropriateness and implementation of care plans. They are required to be independent of the management of the case and of the allocation of resources.

Inter-agency placement

A child looked after by one local authority may be placed for adoption or permanent fostering with adopters or foster carers approved by another adoption or fostering agency.

Kinship care/family and friends/connected persons care

The care of children by relatives or other people well known to the child. This may be on an informal basis or children's services may be involved. The child might be fostered or subject to an order.

Later life letter

A letter written by the child's social worker to the child summarising some of the life story information. For young children, it is information which their adoptive parents will share with them in due course.

Life story work

This is work which should be done with a child by their social worker, in co-operation with their foster carers and their family if possible. Its aim is to give the child as clear a picture as possible of what has happened in their life and why they are now being placed for adoption or fostering. It is an opportunity for the child to express their feelings about what has happened so far. The process of assimilating the information and making sense of it may well take years and the child will need ongoing help and support.

Life story book

A "book" prepared with (or, for infants, for) the child by a social worker, foster carer and/or adoptive parent that documents the child's life, from birth, through his or her life in foster care or residential care, to adoption. It may include a description of the child's birth parent/s and/or birth family, other siblings or half-siblings, where the child was born, foster carers, and how the child became adopted. The purpose of the book is to provide a link for the child (when old enough) with his or her past and life history. The book is given to the adoptive parents who use the information sensitively, with the understanding that it belongs to the child. Where no such book exists, workers or carers can work on completing one with the child.

Looked after – England and Wales

This term includes both children "in care" and accommodated children. Local authorities have certain duties towards all looked after children and their parents, which include the duty to safeguard and promote the child's welfare and the duty to consult with children and parents before taking decisions.

Non-agency adoption

This is where a child has not been placed by an adoption agency. The most common of these circumstances is step-parent adoption where the child is the birth child of one of the applicants. Non-agency adoption applications are sometimes made by grandparents whose grandchild lives with them

Open adoption

This term may be used very loosely and can mean anything from an adoption where a child continues to have frequent face-to-face contact with members of his or her birth family, to an adoption where there is some degree of "openness", e.g. the birth family and adopters meeting each other once. Openness in adoption is best imagined as a continuum from secrecy to unsupervised contact with many options in between. People using the term should be asked exactly what they mean!

Parental responsibility (PR) – England and Wales

Parental responsibility is defined by the Children Act 1989 as 'all the rights, duties, powers, responsibilities and authority which by law a parent of a child has in relation to the child and his or her property'. The most important elements include:

- providing a home for the child;
- having contact with the child;
- protecting and maintaining the child;
- disciplining the child;
- determining and providing for the child's education;
- determining the religion of the child;
- consenting to the child's medical treatment;
- naming the child or agreeing to the child's change of name;
- consenting to or withholding consent to placement for adoption and adoption.

When a child is born to married parents, they share parental responsibility. A child's mother always has parental responsibility. A father who is not married to the child's mother does not automatically have it but may acquire it by formal agreement with the mother, by court order or by jointly registering the birth with the child's mother and being named on the birth certificate. Birth parents can only lose it on the making of an adoption order. When an adoption order is made, parental responsibility passes solely and irrevocably to the adoptive parent(s). Other individuals may acquire parental responsibility by the making of a special guardianship order, when a child is placed for adoption, a guardian in certain circumstances following the death of birth parent(s), a step-parent by agreement with the birth parent(s) or by court order, and a married couple who have a child born by surrogacy providing at least one of them is the genetic parent. Local authorities can acquire parental responsibility by the granting of an emergency protection order, an interim or full care order or a placement order or a formal parental consent to the child's placement for adoption.

Permanent fostering

A placement for a child with a new family, which is planned to be the child's family for life. It is a descriptive term rather than a formal legal status. An adoption order lasts for life. Other court orders, such as a care order or special guardianship order, cease once the child is 18.

Placement order – England and Wales

An order made by the court authorising a local authority to place a child for adoption with any prospective adopters who may be chosen by the authority. It continues in force until it is revoked, or an adoption order is made in respect of the child or the child marries, forms a civil partnership or attains the age of 18. Only local authorities may apply for placement orders.

Prospective Adopter's Report

A report prepared by an adoption agency when it has assessed prospective adopters. Some parts of the UK use Form F for this purpose.

Qualifying determination – England and Wales

In relation to suitability to adopt a child – a determination made by an adoption agency following a recommendation by the adoption panel that it considers a prospective adopter is not suitable to be an adoptive parent and does not propose to approve him/her as suitable.

Reporting Officer

A social worker appointed by a court when a birth parent wishes to consent to the child's placement for adoption, or consent to an adoption order. The Reporting Officer ensures that the parent/s fully understand the legal effect of the consent and have given their consent unconditionally; the Reporting Officer then witnesses the birth parent/s signed consent. After speaking with the Reporting Officer, if one or both of the birth parents decides not to consent to placement or adoption, the local authority will have to apply for a placement order (in England and Wales) or the adopters would have to ask the court to disperse with their consent to the making of the adoption order.

Residence Order – Northern Ireland

A court order that sets out the arrangements as to the person(s) with whom the child is to live. Where a Residence Order is made in favour of someone who does not already have parental responsibility for the child (e.g. a relative or foster carer), that person will acquire parental responsibility subject to certain restrictions (e.g. they cannot consent to the child's adoption). This parental responsibility will only last as

long as long as the Order (which can last until the child's 18th
birthday). A Residence Order discharges a court order. However, a
birth parent with parental responsibility retains this and shares it with
the holder of the Order.

Residence Order allowance – Northern Ireland

Trusts can contribute to the cost of a child's maintenance when the
child is living with someone under a Residence Order, provided he or
she is not living with a parent or step-parent. This financial
contribution is usually referred to as a Residence Order allowance.

Special guardianship order allowance – England and Wales

Special guardians caring for a child previously looked after by a local
authority are entitled to an assessment of their support needs by the
local authority that was responsible for the child. A range of financial
help may be available, from a means-tested one-off payment to a
regular, ongoing allowance. This cannot replace available benefits or
tax credits. The local authority can also help with legal costs or a
settling-in grant to cover required furniture or equipment, which will
not be means-tested.

Stage One – pre-assessment process (England)

This stage of the adoption process in England starts once an agency
has accepted a Registration of Interest from an individual. It should
normally be completed within two months. Should it take longer, it
must be recorded on the prospective adopter's case record. A Stage
One plan should be agreed with the prospective adopter. Initial
training and preparation will be given, and all prescribed checks and
references will be carried out. Where an agency decides that a
prospective adopter is not suitable to adopt during or at the end of
this stage, it must inform them in writing with a clear explanation of

the reasons. Prospective adopters may make a complaint, but have no recourse to the Independent Review Mechanism (IRM).

Stage Two – assessment process (England)

Prospective adopters in England are not able to start this part of the process until they have successfully completed Stage One. Stage Two should take four months to the final decision, unless there are exceptional circumstances or the prospective adopter asks to delay. Reasons should be recorded on the case file. A written Assessment Plan should be prepared with the prospective adopter. This stage covers an assessment of the prospective adopter's suitability to adopt and should include any necessary training. A prospective adopter's report (PAR) is completed, an adoption panel considers the case, and a decision-maker makes a final decision.

Testamentary Guardian

A person who has been formally appointed to act as a child's guardian after the death of the child's birth parent(s). The guardian will acquire parental responsibility. Not to be confused with a children's guardian or a special guardian.

Twin-track/parallel planning

This refers to a situation where work in relation to rehabilitation home to parents, and preliminary work about other permanent options for a child, are done at the same time.

Tia likes...reading, the colour pink and daydreaming!

but most of all Tia would like to be part of a family.

There are thousands of children waiting for an adoptive family, some wait much longer than others. We want to help change that.

To adopt you can be single, married, divorced, in a same sex relationship, working or retired. What you do need is the commitment to offer a child a loving, caring home which they can thrive.

Adoption Matters is a children's charity specialising in adoption, that is all we do and have been doing so for nearly 70 years. We are proud of the award winning* service we offer our adopters, working with council adoption teams across the whole of the UK.

For more information visit:
www.adoptionmatters.org or call us on 0300 123 1066

* The ONLY Voluntary Adoption Agency in the NW to be rated as 'Outstanding' by Ofsted consecutively in 2008, 2011 & 2014. BAAF Voluntary Adoption Agency of the year 2012 & 2014.

adoption matters
A proud history of children's futures

Dear my future family,

I just want you to know that I understand what a big decision I am.

Deciding to love someone like me, to make me a part of your family and help me to grow up into a happy person is a big job and you probably need time to think about whether it's what you really want.

There will be a lot of boring paperwork to do and people will ask you a lot of questions about your life in a way you're not used to and it might feel uncomfortable.

Perhaps you're worried that you won't get chosen to be an adopter and it might break your heart a little bit and that's a scary thought.

So I know that it might be a while before you pick up the phone.

But I know that you will, because I am waiting for you. And I will be here when you're ready.

So will all the friendly people at Caritas Care. They understand.

I will see you soon,
Your future child   x x x

CaritasCare
Making lives better

When you're ready to have a chat, we'll be on the other end of this number...
0800 652 6955

Or this email address...
dutyadoption@caritascare.org.uk

www.caritascare.org.uk
#DearAdopter

If you are wholeheartedly considering adopting - go for it!

Not everyone has 2.4 children. There are many different ways to become a family, and adoption has brought the joys of family life to so many children and parents all over the country. Susan explains why she decided to adopt her daughter, and how it changed her life.

"I've got a birth son of 34 and I have got an adopted daughter who is going to be 11 years old soon. The first day that I met her was on 14th of February, Valentine's day! How good is that? That is something I will never be able to forget.

"She brings so much joy to my life, so much happiness. In all that process of wanting to go through adoption I didn't think, being a single parent, that I would be able to do that, because back in those days it was always a thing of mother and father.

"Approaching Coram, getting an interview straight away – that made me feel comfortable; that made me feel like these are the right people to go with. They have become an extended family to me and to my daughter. Because if there is a need or if you feel that you might be concerned about something, you know that you can pick up the phone and there is always somebody there that can guide you and help you.

"If there is anyone out there that may be thinking about adopting and they might be holding back for one reason or another, don't. If it's something that you really, wholeheartedly are passionate about doing, then I suggest just go for it."

coram
better chances
for children
since 1739

Are you thinking about adoption?

Coram runs a leading independent adoption agency with some of the best success rates in the country. Our experienced teams work in and around London, Cambridgeshire and the East Midlands.

We have been helping children find new parents for more than 40 years and support families through the adoption process and afterwards - for as long as they need us.

Visit **www.coramadoption.org.uk** to find out more.